WHAT TO DO TO
RETIRE
SUCCESSFULLY

WHAT TO DO TO
RETIRE
SUCCESSFULLY

Navigating Psychological, Financial
and Lifestyle Hurdles

MARTIN B. GOLDSTEIN, DO, FACN

New Horizon Press

Far Hills, New Jersey

Requests for permission should be addressed to:
New Horizon Press
P. O. Box 669
Far Hills, NJ 07931

Martin B. Goldstein
    What to Do to Retire Successfully:
    Navigating Psychological, Financial and Lifestyle Hurdles

Cover design: Charley Nasta
Interior design: Scribe Inc.

Library of Congress Control Number: 2014938453

ISBN-13 (paperback): 978-0-88282-486-4
ISBN-13 (eBook): 978-0-88282-487-1

New Horizon Press

Manufactured in the U.S.A.

19   18   17   16   15   1   2   3   4   5

To Gary, Susan, Aaron, Lenny and David:
The next generation
and
To two successful retirees:
Ellen, the love of my life, and Honey, a true sister.

ACKNOWLEDGMENTS

I wish to thank Ellen Goldstein for reading the raw text, assisting with the editing and making many useful suggestions. Throughout this project, her support has been very helpful and greatly appreciated.

AUTHOR'S NOTE

This book is based on the author's research, personal experiences, interviews and real life experiences. In order to protect privacy, names have been changed and identifying characteristics have been altered except for contributing experts.

For purposes of simplifying usage, the pronouns his/her and s/he are sometimes used interchangeably. The information contained herein is not meant to be a substitute for professional evaluation and therapy with mental health professionals.

TABLE OF CONTENTS

Preface   xiii

Chapter 1:   The Psychology of Retirement   1

Chapter 2:   The Practicality of Retirement   33

Chapter 3:   Your Retirement Environment   63

Chapter 4:   Investment Alternatives   77

Chapter 5:   Financial Formulas for Retirement   101

Chapter 6:   Lifestyle in Anticipation of Retirement   111

Chapter 7:   Affluent Behavior Patterns   137

Chapter 8:   Funding for Retirement   157

Chapter 9:   Living Arrangements   173

Chapter 10:   Occupying Yourself in Retirement   199

Epilogue   211

Bibliography   217

Notes   219

PREFACE

This book spells out a step-by-step approach to a successful and contented retirement, including psychological, practical and financial formulas for the best ways to achieve desired goals. I will address the difficulties in adapting to a life after work's end, teaching the adjustment and coping skills required to have a contented retirement.

My approach differs from other books with similar titles by professionally and personally addressing the psychology of retirement, as well as the practical lifestyle and financial aspects, by one who is living it.

First, the physical and psychological foundations for retirement success are explored.

Then, the chapter on practicality deals with various personality types and discusses which are more readily suited to retire comfortably and which would find it more difficult. It also addresses the issues facing those workers who are forced to retire and other factors hampering adjustment to a retired state.

The next three chapters focus on your financial situation. Steps for saving and investing with proper asset allocation at different age periods are stressed. Specific formulas are introduced spelling out the monetary requirements for continuance of a standard of living comparable to times of employment for different income levels. A comprehensive financial handling of retirement resources is outlined.

The lifestyle portion details how to enact a plan for eventual retirement while still working and being concerned with family and life matters.

The last part of the book teaches the actual steps to take to facilitate an easy transition to retired living. Included are funding avenues, decision-making regarding living arrangements and personal insights on rewarding retirement activities.

This comprehensive approach, if applied rigorously, should enable you to retire successfully.

CHAPTER 1

The Psychology of Retirement

Retirement is as much a state of mind as a cessation of the labors of life. It has to be regarded as the culmination of those labors, to be enjoyed and cherished. Sadly, many times this is not the case. People who are abruptly thrust into the untimely loss of a job find themselves adrift and ill-prepared for a future not of their choosing. Therefore, preparation for such a prospect must begin at an early age and with adequate psychological as well as practical and financial preparation.

Not all people must adapt to a retirement lifestyle. Those who have a vast amount of money and the freedom to choose are not the primary concern of this work. I address middle-income workers and professionals who need to save and invest for retirement. These individuals have to transition from a routine of going to work each day to a life of greater relaxation and adjustment to the travails of aging and loss of a work environment.

If one can learn to combine the carefree attitude of one's early years with the wisdom gained through experience, the later years can be the most gratifying of all. This freedom from care does not come by itself—it must be learned and prepared for. Preparation should begin while one is still at the peak of one's earning potential.

The substitute for the work experience has to be addressed early on with both physical and mental preparation.

PHYSICAL ASPECTS

The importance of physical exercise cannot be understated. As health allows, sport activities are important in any retirement regimen. To the amount the body permits, playing a game and working out should be part of any routine. If you can do neither, walking or just rocking in a rocking chair can help. Robust health goes hand-in-hand with a positive attitude.

DIET AND APPEARANCE

The healthy diet that may have been difficult to maintain with the stress of a busy work schedule is now more possible with the greater ease of a retirement schedule. In your retirement years, eating better and keeping active are of prime importance, especially if you dine out more frequently. The maintenance of your desired weight is important for body image acceptance.

Pleasing yourself in appearance goes a long way to bolster self-esteem and radiates attraction. Being comfortable with yourself is of utmost importance in adjusting to your new time of life.

ACTIVITIES

Fulfilling lifelong desires, such as taking more vacations, traveling to interesting places and being involved in activities not possible while working, can help occupy the newfound free time caused by the loss of working hours.

Mental exercise is as important as physical exercise. Being involved with hobbies, whether it's getting into new ones or just being more committed to old ones, is required to stave off boredom. Boredom is the enemy of the retired state and can be avoided by utilizing an anti-boredom system: start off each day with a to-do list and keep busy. Such lists should have a continuing activity, such as when you are writing or constructing something. Whether it's writing letters, articles or books or making furniture, these are engrossing and gratifying activities and gratification is the greatest weapon against boredom.

Read each day. Choose newspapers, e-readers, magazines, journals, books, websites or other material. If you can use your computer or smartphone, be involved with family and friends and have discussions. You have more time to do this now. Challenge your mind with puzzles and quizzes.

Always remember that boredom is your enemy. Fight it!

ACCEPTANCE

Adjustment can be just as easily done as said. Older age demands one adjustment after another. Giving up an activity should always be followed by being involved with another one which is easier to do. If you can no longer lift forty pounds, lift twenty, ten or even five, but don't stop lifting if you can help it. Do not bemoan the fact that you can no longer lift forty pounds. Accept it and move on. There are emotional substitutes. Revel in the fact that you may be smarter or richer than you were when you could lift forty pounds (or some other substitute).

Constantly give yourself encouragement. Be your own therapist. Urge yourself on to do your absolute best at whatever you do while keeping active.

Take advantage of your extra relaxation time and watch your favorite television programs and movies. Go to the theater as often as you can. Being engrossed in lives other than your own broadens your outlook and maintains your interest.

NEW ROLE

Be involved. Whether with hobbies, family, charities, organizations or other group activities, stay active. Don't ever quit on yourself. Remember, as a senior citizen you have life experience to impart to others. Always feel important and contribute when you can. Although your children may feel that at some point they have surpassed you, you still have a lot to teach them and, perhaps even moreso, your grandchildren.

Spread your love and care around. There are others who need those positive emotions from you. At some level you are revered by those close to you. Never denigrate your self-worth and be free to exhibit your knowledge; don't feel rejected if it's not readily accepted. With age they will learn how right you were.

SPIRITUALITY

Retirement should be a time of reflection. It is a time to remember old friends and loved ones by cataloguing photographs and communications; but it is also a time to make some new friends. Be it golfing, card playing, mahjong or book club companions, make new friends. In general, try new things. We must all fight the sense of loss and depression that comes with painful memories and compensate with good times and positive memories. Always grasp onto previous happiness and bring it forward.

If you are inclined, participation in church, temple, synagogue or mosque activities can now be increased. More time is also available for spiritual exercises, like meditation, contemplation, prayer and relaxation techniques like yoga and tai chi, among others.

Build yourself up. You are not older and uglier, you are wiser and perhaps richer. You would not make the same mistakes you did when you were younger, would you? No, you are smarter than you were then. Constantly remind yourself of this.

Keep your spirits up. Don't give in. No matter how sick or frail you become, don't give up hoping for better days to come.

STUDY

Retirement can be a time of learning. Many retirees felt that they could not devote adequate time to study during their work and child-rearing years. Now, with the available time you not only can read more but can attend lectures, enroll in classes and even matriculate at a college, institute or technical school if so desired. That unfulfilled goal to obtain a long-sought-after degree is now possible. Many harbor a love of learning which might not be satisfied in younger years and can be accommodated in later life.

Gaining new knowledge is self-fulfilling and gratifying, especially in a stress-free environment. Not needing to please teachers or worrying about tests or grades, the retiree is free to pursue what he or she wants to learn without any outside constraints. Differing from many prior school experiences, devoid of social and other pressures endured at an earlier age, learning can be a pleasure.

The range of individual desires is endless. One can increase expertise in rebuilding automobile engines, re-experience historical events or enhance skills in scientific or technical areas.

Professionals are taught that, in order to be proficient at their craft, learning should never cease. We must remain students until the end of life. Even teachers should remain students.

Retirement is a wonderful time for learning. The retiree should set aside adequate time to study, not only for self-fulfillment, but also for the gratification of achievement.

SEXUALITY

Nothing gives a sense of youthfulness as much, in my opinion, as an active sex life. Especially in the years after work, a fulfilling physical relationship brings happiness.

In an age group where genital impotence and dryness are routinely more pronounced than in earlier years, adjustments can be made, be they oral or masturbatory, to achieve as frequent an orgasm as desired. This is a physiological as well as a psychological requirement. Glands are meant to secrete for normal functioning.

There are usually no longer young children around to interfere, so with the additional time available and no distractions, sexual activity periods can be planned or spontaneous. In any meaningful relationship, sexual gratification is a proper instinct and should be pleasurable in retirement.

GOALS

Just as you did during your working years, set goals for your retirement years. Don't just retire *from* something, retire *to* something. Whether it's taking certain vacations, such as visiting exotic countries, climbing a mountain, basking in the sun at the beach or on the deck of a cruise ship, fulfill your goals. Visit cities to which you've never been before, even if they are just across your home state. Get up and go!

Don't procrastinate. Time is no longer on your side. If you are in a new relationship, don't dilly-dally. See each other as often as possible. Remember, a date each day for six weeks is as much time together as younger people get to experience in a whole year.

If you have been left alone due to a partner's death, attempt to fill that void. Try going online and visiting dating websites. Have family and friends introduce you to new people. Go to places that cater to singles your age.

Cultivate new experiences. Try new games and activities. Go to that stadium you've always dreamed about to see an event of your choosing. Be involved with people, art, sports, music, etc. to your taste. Retirement can be a time of ambition, a time to experience things not possible when work and family matters prevented them.

EXPRESSION

For many, retirement may be the freest time of their lives. Retired people are able to pursue whatever they wish as never before: no parents to answer to and usually no children to physically care for. Now you can seek your heart's desire, no matter how outlandish or bewildering it may seem to others. Go to Paris and paint. Build model railroads or doll houses. As long as you are able, go fishing twice a week. Go to a dude ranch and ride a horse, go to Egypt and ride a camel or go to India and ride an elephant. Just loll around the house and grill burgers in your backyard. You can do anything you want. There are no bosses, no supervisors and no schedules to meet—only those of your own choosing.

Embrace this freedom. Enjoy it. Relish it. Understand that you own it and count it among your blessings.

AGING

Aging means giving up youthful activities. One by one, a lack of previous abilities necessitates the giving up of something. Physical pursuits have to be curtailed and adjustments have to be made. The best adjustment is to replace an inability with a new activity. If you can no longer play tennis, take up ping pong or another pursuit. If you cannot go for long walks or jog, ride a bicycle. Do something new to replace something lost.

If old friends and family members have moved or passed away, find new ones. Never engage in self-pity; move on. Don't feel sorry for yourself. You have reached a stage of life others have failed to achieve. You are a survivor. There is too little time left to spend weighed down by guilt.

Accept your retirement as a reward well deserved. Treat it as a new job. Do things to make yourself proud. When younger members of your family promote their achievements, trot out yours. Keep striving within your scope of mind and abilities. Don't ever quit on yourself.

END GAME

In the United States, in our competitive culture, work has been glorified beyond what is felt in more relaxed societies. In many American circles, retirement has been denigrated to be just a time to wait for death.

Those of us who have enjoyed a much more wonderful experience can readily present a different point of view. Those who choose to embrace retirement should feel that it is a glorious time to do what one wants, as often as one wants, how and when and where one wants, without any stigmatization.

Death should also be embraced. Depending on your religious beliefs, whether you fancy going to heaven, being reincarnated into a higher caste or simply entering a final period of rest and peace, embrace it. Live your retirement days as if each day is your last one and have as much fun and enjoyment as you can.

Never dwell on death. It will eventually come. However, don't fear it. Embrace it as an ending of all worries and tribulations: a resting in peace and contentment.

EMOTIONAL ASPECTS

Don't get agitated. Take it easy. You have arrived. Be proud of yourself. Tolerable regimens can lead to new victories. You should feel like a winner. Losing is deflating; accept the challenge of this period of life and treat yourself like a winner.

Every life is filled with mistakes, failures and misfortunes. Do not dwell on the negative. Focus on the good times and positive aspects. Revel in the victories and the successes. Congratulate yourself on overcoming the difficulties. Do this with self-forgiveness and with a strong sense of self-promotion. Retirement is a victory over the pitfalls of labor, over the trials of aging and family and over the maze of life's changes.

Be victorious in your outlook. Be serene. Be less eager to get angry, less prone to judge and less likely to be offended by criticism. Realize that there are some who criticize indiscriminately to cover up their own insecurities. You have arrived at the pinnacle of living. Enjoy it.

Do not think about what you don't have or have not accomplished and accept what you do have and appreciate it. No one bats a thousand; even the best baseball hitters get on base less than forty percent of the time. A winning attitude is the best answer to any downturn. Love who you are. You must love yourself before you can love anyone else.

Retirement should not be an end, but the beginning of a new chapter of life. Look forward to retirement with anticipation.

TRANSITIONAL PHASE

No matter how traumatic the circumstance necessitating retirement, be it an illness or an unwanted termination of employment, adequate preparation can reduce the severity of the blow. Preparation is the key.

During your working years, unless you have great job security like owning a growing business in a recession-proof industry, prepare for the worst-case scenario. As technology is replacing manpower with the growing use of robotics and other modalities, job security in the future will not be what it was in the past.

Adequately preparing for a smooth transition is the key to easing into a successful retirement. This can be accomplished by utilizing the formulas for success outlined later in this book.

WORRY

Health issues and financial concerns are among the most common causes for worry, along with familial disruptions. Illnesses can come at any time and are dependent on environmental, genetic or traumatic precipitants and their prevention is usually difficult or nearly impossible to plan for. However, during the retirement period, with a more laid-back attitude and a relaxed approach devoid of rushing, stressing and needing to push boundaries, one can limit one's exposure to the elements that trigger the usual maladies of advanced age. One is now free enough not to have to brave severely inclement weather and to always be properly dressed to go outdoors. Do not rush. Falling, with resulting injuries, can be life-threatening. Always watch where you are walking, so you will not trip and fall. Whenever it is possible, walk in a timely fashion; do not run.

As a matriarch or patriarch of your family, you may be called upon to arbitrate family disputes. You know your family members, so either use your sagacity to give advice or decline as you see fit. Remember, in your advanced age and need, you may have to depend on these same people in the future, so be wise about it. You do not wish to alienate someone you will need later on. Tread lightly in any judgment. The old adage to say nothing if you can't say something nice is even more on point as you grow older.

The one thing that you can remove, or at the very least markedly reduce, from your worry list is your financial future. Unlike your health and family matters, you can, with careful planning, control the monetary events leading to a bright outlook, not only for yourself, but possibly for your heirs as well. Adhering to the formulas outlined in this book will typically result in achieving financial security that can lead to a worry-free retirement, no matter your income bracket.

RELATIONSHIPS

With over half the marriages in the United States ending in divorce, family makeup has become, in many cases, more complex. Often, this complexity has led to division, jealousy and animosity among family members. Coupling this additional negative element to the usual disagreements among members of intact families, familial strife is quite a common occurrence. As one who has conducted family therapy sessions for many years, I can attest to the viciousness and hatred that can fester between people who at one time felt love for each other. Retirement should be a time of peace-making and a time to set aside differences and propose a truce to all hostilities. The mind should be cleansed of negative feelings. You are above bad-mouthing anyone; it is beneath your status now. You have arrived at a level beyond petty grievances. All feuding and ill-will should be shed like a worn-out coat, not only for the tranquil results but for the peace of mind and pride it will instill.

MARRIAGE

Nothing can be as disruptive to retirement planning as an unstable marriage. Knowing you have married someone who will be a trustworthy partner through good times and bad is a gift beyond words. I have been blessed to have been married to the same good woman for over fifty years. However, despite this very stable marriage, I can tell you it has taken a lot of emotional effort on both our parts to make it work. We are only human. We are not angels. There are no perfect people and adjustments have to be made to accommodate a happy union.

A couple's retirement needs to be a unified action, with both partners fully committed and ready to share responsibilities. Each partner should be acquainted with financial and other obligations to be able to take over day-to-day leadership should the other become incapacitated or pass away.

Today, many couples are choosing cohabitation over formal marriage. This, along with multiple marriages and complex families, complicates estate planning and retirement goals. These issues will be addressed later in much greater detail, but one should always be adequately represented legally and financially by professionals in these matters. Otherwise, the results can be catastrophic. Binding prenuptial agreements can protect against threatened retirement assets and should be considered whenever there is a substantial difference in the wealth of the two uniting parties, especially when there are other potential heirs already in place.

Do not jeopardize any sizeable retirement benefits on the whim of a love feeling you experience in older age, something you may feel you have never had before. Remember the geriatric years are the years when the past is measured against the future as never before. You are more prone to reminisce about missed chances and lost romances than you did in younger times. You are also more apt to fall for romantic folly. The ancient adage "There's no fool like an old fool" bears witness to the truism of this warning. In many ways this is the most vulnerable time of your life, both mentally and physically. Do not be taken in by a misplaced longing for something that is not real and can be devastating to your future.

VICTIMIZATION

Always remember that if you are aging and have accumulated an enviable nest egg, you are a tempting target for charlatans. Some criminals specialize in robbing or vandalizing the elderly and infirmed. Try never to place yourself in harm's way. Do not be alone or in deserted or out-of-the-way places. Be wary of schemes or strangers offering unsolicited help. Heed the wise axiom: "If it sounds too good to be true, it probably is." Don't become a victim. Physical or financial harm can be catastrophic to retirement plans. The psychological trauma of abuse or neglect in older individuals can be more debilitating than in younger people, who can bounce back more easily. The resultant depression can be devastating.

LIVING ARRANGEMENTS

Safety should also be a factor in choosing where to live after retirement. This is especially important if one is alone or suffering from illness. Health and self-reliant abilities should determine whether to stay in an apartment, single home, duplex, retirement community or nursing facility. Unfortunately, in cases of extreme disability, family members are often required to make these choices and sometimes not in the best interest of the retiree.

Moving in with friends or relatives can become complicated, with disagreements over the division of chores and financial obligations. After doing things a certain way for many years, the adjustment to the habits of others can be annoying and lead to displeasure and disharmony. Know yourself. If you do not readily adapt to accommodate the desires of others and have had bad experiences attempting to do so in the past, do not obligate yourself to live with others. No matter how much you love your children and grandchildren, if at all possible do not move in with them. Having spent many hours in family therapy sessions with unhappy family members, I can attest to the truth of the old saying that "Familiarity breeds contempt."

ADJUSTMENTS

The later years of life test our ability to overcome the cruelties of the aging process. One by one we are called upon to give up cherished activities and people we love and admire. It is a time of trying our resilience as we never have before. It is a time of pain, a time of loss and a time of such despair to some people. It is a time when we may have to rely more on others than at any other period since early childhood. It is a time when we are robbed of our strength, our vitality, our good looks and vanity and are left only to recall the memories of these precious things taken from us. However, it can also be a time wherein we muster sufficient energy to retain hope for the pleasures yet to come: victories yet to be won, birthdays yet uncelebrated, weddings yet to be danced at, books still unread, movies and plays yet unseen and music yet unheard. If we cannot dance at those weddings, we can stand or sit at the side of the dance floor and clap. In what time is left to us, we must go on in joy, despite our pain and disabilities. We can conquer the adversity of old age with a sense of good purpose, with courage and conviction in our ability to overcome the ravages of aging.

REFLECTIONS

As more of life lies behind than in front, there is more to recall than to anticipate and subsequently memories capture more of the thinking hours, especially in a leisure-oriented environment. Daydreaming also becomes more frequent when there is additional time to spend with one's inner self. The long-suppressed questions that continue to nag on beg attention. What would have been had I done this instead of that? If I had chosen another path from the one I did go down? Second-guessing is the fool's errand of a mind with time to waste. When time is relatively short, time is a precious commodity not to be wasted in useless supposition. Live well with the choices you have made. They were the best you could do given the circumstances, your background and what you were comfortable with at the time. We all make good and bad choices during a lifetime. The success lies, as with all things, in the percentages and the balance the choices create. As long as they tilt toward the positive, as most likely they do to have gotten you to this point, be satisfied with yourself and do not dwell on what might have been. Had you chosen differently, things could be much worse.

In contrast to obsessive thinking about possible mistakes, focus on the most successful things in your life: your family, your achievements and the happiest moments of your existence.

REGRESSION

It is natural to consider retirement to be a return to a form of childhood. Old age has often been called "a second childhood." In the worst sense it means to focus on the childlike senility of seniors, with loss of memory, decrease in bodily functions and sometimes questionable behavior; but in the best of cases, the ones we strive for, it means reaching a plateau of contentment, what some call *Nirvana*. In ancient Sanscrit, Nirvana means "a blowing out": the blowing out of senseless striving, of useless competition, of the need for envy and wishing harm to befall others and instead reaching the degree of security of a happy childhood.[1] This is the goal of a life based on the attainment of serenity, not merely achievement. The greatest achievers may be unhappy and unfulfilled in other aspects of their lives, while those who seek out the road to self-gratification in harmony with their environment gain the solace of peace.

In all of your endeavors, an avenue of moderation—avoiding extremes—appears to be the proper path to a contented later life, after labor's end.

There is no crime in catering to the inner child, present in all of us, when we no longer need to hide the craving for this indulgence. Wishes can now become realities. Previous deprivations need no longer occur. Goals can be met, strivings fulfilled, wrongs corrected and overdue obligations given attention to. The personal world, which might have seemed to be going in the wrong direction, can be made right again.

LOVE

It goes without saying that love is the most important human emotion. Often overused, the word love is attached to inanimate objects as well as people. In many societies humans have sometimes come to love things more than people. This is particularly true in persons who have been hurt and disappointed by those close to them, particularly when they were young and formulating their relationships to others.

The damage caused by painful experiences in the prototypical relationships with parents and surrogates can lead to an inability to fully trust or relate properly, even to a love object. A resultant psychological armor can then engulf the individual so as to not allow that closeness of spirit that is required in true caring. The sensitivity required to appreciate the feelings of others is then lessened to the point, at times, of inflicting hurt and in the extreme even harm, with little or no care.

Without even considering sociopathy, we have to address the hardening of feelings that may occur in a life filled with perceived disappointment, failure and perhaps even cruelty. These psychological deficiencies, undetected and unaddressed in earlier times of avoidance and repression, might, with greater self-awareness, be brought to one's attention and treated. Even people who merely unintentionally have neglected those who are close to them due to work distraction might, in retirement, seek professional help to overcome these causes of love blockage. Retirement, in these cases, may be a time to consider getting individual or couples counseling in order to improve, or even save, those relationships.

Having spent a sizeable portion of my career administering geriatric psychiatric care, I can attest to the value of psychotherapy, as well as the usual medicinal therapy required in the treatment of older patients. Many adjustment difficulties of the retirement period can be worked out, gaining emotional improvement with proper therapy.

Everyone deserves to be able to enjoy and appreciate true love during their lifetimes. It is the right and privilege of every human being. To not have experienced it in one form or another, be it love of a partner, family member, cherished work or devoted cause, is a psychological deficit and leaves a void. To have reached the retirement age without having experienced it due to an intra-psychic blockage is a condition that may be treatable; therapy is advised. The old saying "Love makes the world go around" is self-explanatory in describing how romantics feel about this emotion. Without love there is no sense of true caring, no feeling of completeness, no exhilaration of spirit.

Some find a substitute in religion or devotion to a cause to compensate for lack of person-to-person commitment, but without love there is an undeniable emptiness. Unfortunately, I have encountered this suffering in the psychotherapy of older, usually depressed, patients, who feel a loss of love, being ignored or neglected.

SAFETY

Having lived a life to the point of being able to no longer need to work to earn a living usually means that there has also been an accumulation of the trappings of wealth: pieces of art, furs, jewelry, valuable coins and the like, bought or inherited over a lifetime. These may be precious to their owners because of the memories and associations attached to them, besides their monetary value. They are also the target of burglars. Homes with such valuables should be adequately insured and protected with burglar alarms. The loss of the life of a loved one is the most devastating of losses, but the loss of objects of attachment which may have come to represent such a loss can also be a cruel blow and has to be protected against. While affection for non-living items has been denigrated as misplaced caring, those who have become enamored with such memorabilia can be severely hurt by a criminal intrusion, especially when these items are representations of important events and barriers against loneliness.

PETS

If one does not enjoy a robust social life, retirement can lead to long hours of loneliness. This can readily be abated with the companionship of a faithful animal friend or even a few. The petting of a dog or cat can bring calm and has been reported to lower blood pressure. An old adage states that "Anyone who doesn't think you can buy love has never visited a pet store." To couples who are suffering from "empty nest syndrome," the adoption of an affectionate animal can, in some way, impart a feeling of substitution to soothe parental needs. Walking and romping with a dog can reprise earlier adventures of pleasure and joy and aid in recapturing the carefree attitude of long ago. A loving pet, for many, can be a suitable companion during retirement.

WISH-FULFILLMENT

Recently much media attention has been drawn to the "bucket list" or the things we want to do before we die, perhaps unusual experiences we had no time for or frankly were too ashamed or too fearful to attempt before. Well, retirement is a time of bravery, a time to set shame aside, a time of adventure, to be free enough to go where you have not dared to go before. You no longer have to worry about what others may think or say. If you have had a previously hidden desire to do something, go ahead and do it. There is no longer anything or anyone to fear, no scolding or meaningful retribution for any legal undertaking that doesn't harm someone else.

Be brave enough to fulfill your heart's desire. Retirement is the perfect time to set aside previous inhibitions.

CONTEMPLATION

With added free time, it is only natural to expect that there will be periods spent away from other people by oneself. Existential philosophers have decried the absence of self-awareness in modern society. People are generally so involved with their work and others that there remains little time and effort spent in self-examination. Many go through life not truly knowing themselves, what they want, what they like and what their potentials really are. Some spend a lifetime pleasing others and becoming what other people want them to be. They never truly find themselves and never understand who they really are. Retirement can be a time to rectify this absence of self-awareness, a time to find oneself, to no longer just be what one does, but to learn who one is. What are your true wants and desires, not the ones you have been indoctrinated into? The finding of oneself is necessary to complete the personality and gain perspective on the requirements for the pursuit of happiness.

LANGUAGE

It has often been said that communication is the basis of all lasting relationships and the basic ingredient of communication between people is still language. Despite all of the relatively recent advancements in electronic devices with their unique vernacular inventions, no matter what the form it's still just a modification of language. How one speaks and addresses others may go a long way to define the nature of relationships formed prior to and during the retirement phase of life. If you have had difficulties in previous interpersonal doings with other people, perhaps a reassessment of the status of your communicating skills should be undertaken. If you have been a boss and are used to giving orders, understand that your peers are no longer underlings and a different tone and demeanor is now more proper. A demanding stature often causes rebellion and resultant dissent. In a time of greater relaxation and with less need for competition, the rule should be to moderate language vehemence and invoke a sense of kindness and compassion in all wordage.

In general, you should realize that you are no longer experiencing the stress of previous competitive existence and can afford to be more generous and benevolent in your endeavors. This is best expressed in the modulation of speech to convey the concern you have for other people and for their points of view. Even if you feel that your educational or life experience superiority places your opinion above that of another, treat the exuberance and brashness of someone junior to you with the same respect you would wish for yourself. Retirement should be a period of a newfound kindness, perhaps one you have never exhibited before. Remember that "goodness is its own reward" and it pays multiple dividends in advanced age. Speak softly, give advice to others and reap the respect you deserve.

FORGIVENESS

It has been suggested that maturity comes when one forgives one's parents. You mature by forgiving the insults of childhood. In the course of a lifetime a person encounters many painful unpleasantries perpetrated by unthinking or uncaring individuals, some malicious, others unintended but just as hurtful. Over the years, resentments build up. If the insults come from those with sufficient authority to prevent adequate response, it is only natural that significant resentment will occur. If this happens with great frequency, resentment will increase to hatred. Many grow to hate those whom they should normally love or at least like or admire. These painful memories can fester for many years and sometimes transcend death. The pain is deepest when the perceived perpetrator is a person who should have been a protector and guardian against such afflictions. The frustration can build up to a point where the negativity overwhelms the personality and by ego projection the traits of mistrust and unpleasantness are felt by others. Behind every mean and nasty individual there is a story of mistreatment of some kind. Viciousness begets viciousness. This demands that the *golden rule* of treating everyone like you would like to be treated yourself should be the basis of civilized behavior. However, as we have all experienced, this is not always the case.

The relative tranquility of the retired state is the perfect time to reassess the inner disturbances of long-held feelings of anger and frustration and the desire for the now usually impossible retribution against those who we feel have wronged us. This is a time to forgive even that which we cannot forget and to rise above all the painful memories, to aspire to a level to which we could not ascend before.

Let us also recall that the last years are those that may take us closer to whatever maker we believe in. If there is a life hereafter, as many believe, let us not bring our hatred and animosities with us into whatever further existence awaits us. Let us clear our consciences of the venom of the unforgiving. Retirement should begin with a clean slate, unencumbered by the negativity of the past, to be that successful and truly happy period we all deserve.

SIMPLIFICATION

The best avenue to take to an easy transition into a retired state is the simplest one. Get rid of all the unnecessary accoutrements of what you have experienced previously. Reduce numerous homes to just one or two at most. Replace a large house with a smaller one which requires less upkeep. Reduce or totally eliminate house staff. Find ways to save on expenses. If you have to retire on a tight budget, make a list of all non-essential expenditures and stop making purchases you can no longer afford. Living within your means is the hallmark of adequate preparation and execution of retirement. Giving up unneeded luxuries is the price that needs to be paid for the freedom of a low-income retirement.

Hopefully, the readers of this book will heed the advice imparted herein and will not need to sacrifice at all, but be able to maintain the same standard of living or even better in retirement as before. This should be possible for a great majority of middle-income individuals who begin to implement the formulas outlined in this book at a relatively young age. Adequate preparation is the key to a carefree retirement.

ANATOMY

During the course of over forty years of listening to patients in psychotherapy and psychoanalysis sessions I have heard many people, both male and female, express displeasure with parts of their physical features as well as their emotional unhappiness. Many times the two are related. Coming to peace with who you are physically as well as mentally is an important prerequisite for the acceptance of retirement. Many, if not most, people wish that they looked better to themselves. The list of desired improvements is long. With aging, the list grows longer.

You must learn to accept yourself and a chosen partner as you are in totality, especially in a new environment where you might be called upon to spend more time together. With aging, the deficits we are unhappy with may become increased, calling for additional levels of adjustment.

My wife looks as good to me as some movie stars her age. Beauty is in the eye of the beholder. So are wrinkles, blemishes and deformities, which are usually magnified with the aging process. Hair is lost, muscles sag, skin droops and wrinkles—it all comes with the territory. Accept it and move on.

If you can afford to change some of it and you want to do this through cosmetic surgery or similar modalities like botox injections, go right ahead. However, you need to accept and live with the results. Make peace with who you are and with whom you live. This is of paramount importance during retirement when you have the extra time available to look at yourself in the mirror and at your partner.

SICKNESS

Serious illness is a threat to any retirement plan. While pre-existing chronic disability can be adapted to, an acute attack that leads to longtime or permanent disability can be most disruptive. However, the effects even of such disastrous conditions can be miti-gated with adequate planning. As is affordable, the best healthcare insurance, just like homeowners and automobile insurance, must be acquired to prevent financial and even legal difficulties. Greater specifics will be discussed in the financial planning section.

One of the events that cannot be foretold nor emotionally prepared for is the debilitating illness of a loved one. One can only be financially prepared with adequate insurance (long-term for chronic illness requiring nursing care) and if this is not affordable then be prepared to become a caregiver, which taxes any relation-ship. No effort should be spared in obtaining the best medical care.

As we age, we require routine medical supervision. Periodic medical checkups are advised, even in individuals with no symp-toms of disease. In those cases with specific known illnesses, the proper specialist should be consulted, preferably one with experi-ence in handling older patients. An example would be the consul-tation of an endocrinologist to outline the treatment for a patient with diabetes. Doctors who specialize in a specific area of med-icine are usually more familiar with the latest advancements in their specialties and can make more knowledgeable recommenda-tions than those who do not specialize. Ask your family physician to recommend a specialist or go online and check out the creden-tials of specialists in your area.

In cases of severe disease or where a serious treatment regi-men is advised always get a second opinion. Physicians are not gods, although some act as if they are. They make mistakes and, when the stakes are high, never hesitate to seek out a second or even a third opinion as to the proper course of therapy. If cancer is suspected it might be advisable to consult more than one cancer center and get the opinion of several oncologists, if time allows and the resultant delay is not life-threatening. Except in emergencies or life-threatening situations, whenever surgery is advised for a geriatric person a second opinion is advised. Older patients are more prone to have post-operative complications and surgery should be avoided whenever possible. In many cases, alternative therapies can be found which may yield comparable results to surgical intervention. An example would be the implementation of physical therapy in lieu of orthopedic surgery in appropriate situations.

DEATH

While the analysis of successful retirement focuses on the joy of living, it also has to include the ultimate prospect of the end of life and the most tolerable emotional response to that eventuality. Earlier in this book I called for embracing the thought process of a peaceful end and rest for oneself, but we must also include the response to the death of a loved one. When two lives have been entwined for a long time, such a loss can be overwhelming. Yet it is an undeniable fact that in any relationship one partner will die first and the other will be left to grieve and carry on alone. In retirement, where the two people usually spend more time together than before and get used to spending quality time together, the separation is more painful, especially if death comes suddenly.

In my many years of treating patients with varied therapies for different psychiatric disorders, I have been called upon to administer to some in the solemn state of impending death and also to their family members. The psychotherapy of death and dying is called thanatologic therapy. In 1969 the Swiss-born psychiatrist Elisabeth Kubler-Ross introduced the concept that there are five stages that

people go through during a terminal illness: denial, anger, bar-
gaining, depression and acceptance. While I have experienced all
of these emotions in dying patients, not all patients seem to go
through all these phases and not necessarily in the order presented.

In my experience, while there is some glimmer of hope for
recovery, the best anti-depressive psychotherapy is to engage the
patient in active exercises to marshal internal forces and attempt
to combat the disease process. This draws one's attention to the
hope for improvement and away from focusing on the emotions
associated with hopelessness. In giving the patient a sense of being
involved actively in the healing process, concentration is not only
redirected from the dangers of the moment, but in admittedly rare
cases remissions have thus been catalyzed. In any event, instilling
hope whenever the inevitable is still in doubt is good medicine.
When the condition grows so grave that the prognosis is no longer
hopeful, a different approach is indicated. I have had the best
results—if such a phrase is applicable in this context—with promotion of reassurance. Presenting the positive aspects of reaching
some sort of paradise, uniting with beloved departed souls, becoming closer to God (for believers) and just emphasizing the end
of pain and the attainment of the peace and serenity of eternal rest
in honest repetition can bring relief and solace to those approaching
life's end. Those people who believe in some form of reincarnation
or soul migration can be consoled by reinforcing such beliefs at the
time of impending demise. In all cases, describing some sort of
positive future, even if it's just of eternal sleep, can be of comfort in
overcoming the fear of approaching death.

GRIEVING

One of the most common quandaries after death is what is considered to be a reasonable time period to express grief before resuming
an active social life. This is certainly an individual decision to be

reached separately by each widow or widower. However, it must be cautioned that in advanced age the future is short and time becomes a precious commodity. Extended grieving, no matter how close the lost relationship was, will not bring the deceased back. Loss can only be compensated for with new gain of some comparable sort, as soon as is feasible. Replacement is also a potent deterrent to the onset of clinical-level depression.

DIVORCE

In some ways and in some cases, divorce can be psychologically equated to a form of death. It is certainly the death of a marriage. From a financial point of view, divorce can be a retirement killer. This will be dealt with in greater detail later in this book; however, the psychological aspects of divorce can definitely be a deterrent to the ideal retirement we all crave. Divorce, prior to or after retirement, drives the average middle-class family to a position of instability wherein retirement plans are usually partially or totally disrupted. Besides the financial catastrophe, animosity is built up by the cause of the estrangement, be it neglect, infidelity, personality clash, money matters, sexual incompatibility or any of the myriad of other reasons people no longer wish to live together. A grave emotional price is paid, akin to that experienced with death. No matter how desired, as in the case of abuse, addiction or both, the sense of a loss of caring, being left alone to be responsible for all matters previously shared leaves many frightened and bewildered. Having to return to the workplace, particularly if the job is not pleasurable or gratifying, is another source of anger and resentment. Needing to go back to a single lifestyle after many years of cohabitation can also be daunting.

In almost all cases where retirement is a desired option in later life, if the union is in jeopardy I strongly advise family counseling of some sort. Seek out your clergyman or, if you can afford it, a professionally trained mental health counselor with experience in this area. If some form of illness is involved, psychiatric consultation is highly advised to aid in the adjustment process.

Emotions often run wild and trump practicality; therefore, the intervention of third party professional objectivity is definitely necessary when rash moves are being contemplated in older-age couples, threatening to destroy what has taken a lifetime to create. Do not overturn the planning of many years with what may turn out to be nothing more than a change-of-life fling. While such ego-boosting moves are commonplace among the very wealthy (who can easily afford such maneuvers), divorce in average-income older people can ruin retirement plans. If at all possible, make every effort to save your union. If there is a threat to your staying together, plan events that promote togetherness, like getaways to places that have special meaning in the history of your relationship (such as where you met or honeymooned).

It may sound as if I am placing a greater value on monetary well-being than on happiness, but understand I am expressing beliefs from the perspective of many years of delving into analysis of the lives of people who wish that they had used sound judgment instead of acting on temporary romantic whims. This is not to say that some unions are just not salvageable and that one or both partners would be better off apart, seeking new arrangements. However, as I've conveyed, from the perspective of preserving a decent retirement, avoid separation if at all possible.

DEPRESSION

The aging process itself is a natural precipitator of depression. Aging is a time of loss and the loss of vitality or loved ones is a common reason people become depressed.

I want to delineate between the unhappiness many feel in the geriatric years, a depression caused in reaction to an unpleasant situation, and endogenous depression, which is an intrapsychic disorder (that is, it comes from within, biological or genetic in nature rather than event-driven), usually requiring pharmacologic and in severe cases somatic therapy as well as psychotherapy. Some severe cases of geriatric depression can also require medication, but many, if not most, cases of depressive reaction to the disabilities associated with growing older can be treated with talk therapies.

The loss of work itself can trigger a depressive response in individuals who have come to depend upon the work environment to be a surrogate family, especially when more time and emotional energy are exerted there than at home. In such cases, loss of work is equated to loss of family and can result in separation anxiety and depression. In the most dramatic cases, suicidal ideation can be associated with having to face a non-regimented future. An existence devoid of definitive structure can be frightening to those who have become so used to such an existence as to not be able to envision a life without it. That is what sometimes makes the retired policeman kill himself and career criminals commit crimes just to be re-incarcerated. In advanced societies we have been so indoctrinated with the work ethic that after decades of being employed and befriending coworkers (sometimes making them our closest or only friends), being deprived of this existence can cause feelings of sadness.

There are varying degrees of depression associated with the older years, sometimes exacerbated by the loss of the employment environment. Symptoms can range from feelings of sadness to extreme withdrawal and bouts of weeping. Withdrawal can be manifested in a loss of interest in things previously enjoyed, isolation from family and friends, a loss of libido or, at worst, suicidal ideation. Those who voice suicidal thoughts openly should always be taken for professional care. Never downplay suicidal remarks. Most people who attempt suicide have spoken to someone about such feelings before trying to harm themselves.

Psychotherapy should focus on the learning and psychological incorporation of the skills of adjustment to a life after work.

ACCOMMODATION

Whether you are the victim of downsizing, have been fired for cause, have become disabled, have run into the age barrier of the charter of a firm, have been offered a severance package from a company or government agency or simply have realized you can't or just don't want to do the job anymore, retirement is a compromise with reality. Like the baseball pitcher with a sore arm who has lost his velocity and the football running back who has an injured leg, the time has come to make the psychological accommodation to a new phase of life. For some this will be easy but for others it may be much more difficult.

In my experience, those individuals who have chosen to work in industries where there is usually a seasonal break or layoff, like school teachers and construction workers, adapt more readily to retirement regimens. Also, those people who are not intimately involved with the intricacies of the work they do, who may be marginal to decisions regarding their status and therefore have little emotional attachment to the work or have never focused in on one career choice but have moved on from one job to another with periods of being idle and collecting unemployment benefits and, later on, Social Security payments, have relatively little difficulty adapting to a retired lifestyle. When the job you do is only a means of making a living and the people you are associated with at work are just casual acquaintances, leaving for a more relaxed environment is no big deal, if you have enough money. The difficulty comes when you don't have enough money.

The psychological concern arises with workers whose lives have become so entwined with the regimentation of their work, sometimes to the detriment of family and other aspects of their lives, that they just don't ever want to quit and don't know when it's time to "throw in the towel."

The process I call *deregimentation* to aid the marginal cases, who can then overcome their difficulties and enjoy a peaceful retirement, will be covered in the *Practicality* chapter of this book. Attention will also be given to individuals who should not choose voluntary retirement.

Be aware that various emotional aspects of retirement can become the exhilarating highs of a carefree existence or the throes of despair if not adequately prepared for.

Hopefully, if the advice and formulas given in this book are adhered to, the reader will experience what I have, a delicious icing on the cake of life.

CHAPTER 2

The Practicality of Retirement

Not all people in a position to choose should consider retiring. Workers who are obligated to retire at a certain age or because of their physical inability to perform their duties properly may have no choice. Neither do those individuals whose positions are superseded by technological changes in their industries.

WHO SHOULD RETIRE AND WHO SHOULDN'T

The questions to be considered are: Are you ready and what will you do after you are no longer employed? Can you afford to retire? Do you want to retire? Have you properly prepared for retirement? Are you psychologically ready to change your life?

The best answers to these questions can be found in self-awareness, because ultimately the answer must come from the individual and how well he or she knows him or herself. How much is your life tied to your work? Do you have sufficient activities and hobbies to sustain your interests? Many people go through stages of their adult lifetime unaware of who they truly are. Bound up in obligations to others, they have consciously or unconsciously suppressed their own true desires in fulfilling their duties to occupation and family. They have become what they do and not who they are. The more you know yourself, the easier it will be to make retirement decisions.

If you have insufficient funds, find yourself unemployed and cannot sustain yourself on unemployment benefits, the answer is simple: you must try to get another job, even if it means retraining in a different industry or starting a business, no matter how humble. These are simplistic solutions to devastating situations and age or infirmity may make them impossible. In conditions such as these, retirement is not even a consideration. However, in this book we will address the positions, needs and desires of those individuals who do have a reasonable choice to make and the ability to do so. To continue working or not? To start a new venture or drift into a state of continual vacation?

There are many aspects involved in the assessment of one's state of preparedness for retiring and we will explore them.

PRIDE

I shall never forget an experience I had many years ago while on vacation in Florida. While strolling through a marina, admiring the large boats docked there, I came upon an older man polishing the chrome rails running along the bow of a huge yacht and crying. I asked him what was wrong. Could I be of any help? He told me he had made a terrible mistake. A year earlier, he said, he sat at the head of a large table in a New York City office as the chairman of the board of a company he had helped to create. He was a "somebody." Now, a year later, after taking voluntary retirement and ceding his power to another, he considered himself a "nobody," doing the work of a deckhand, polishing chrome. He had believed that devoting himself to the object of his vacation time, his yacht, would bring him the joy he sought, not understanding that his prime pleasure was in administering to his real "baby," his business. This sense of loss of self-pride and the admiration of others brought this still-vital man to a point of depression. He was not ready to relinquish the reins of power that had been the source of his pride.

Despite being well educated and affluent, this gentleman had insufficient insight into who he really was and what his personality makeup required for contentment at that time of his life.

PERSONALITY TYPES

Personality can predetermine one's relationship to work: the degree of motivation, the amount of enjoyment in accomplishment, the attachment to the work milieu, the camaraderie felt toward fellow workers and the ability to easily (or with difficulty) exit this existence.

Compulsive individuals who readily become regimented, adhere to the discipline of the workplace and are prone to over-evaluate the fact of accomplishment may find it more difficult to leave familiar surroundings, while those who are more easygoing and apt to consider work as a means to an end may find it easier to transition to retired status.

Dependent individuals may, for various reasons—a lack of a social existence outside of the workplace, a need to replace an unpleasant home environment or the creation of a surrogate familial existence—find it difficult to divorce themselves from the work atmosphere. Whereas those people who are more independent, perhaps more used to working by themselves, especially the ones who create their own tasks and are capable of setting their own boundaries, are usually more readily adaptable to retirement. No matter how involved with other matters, the retirement years are usually more isolated than the working ones and, the more an individual enjoys his or her own company, the more gratifying this can be. This is not to denigrate the joy of companionship offered in retirement homes and villages.

Workaholics, those who relish work beyond all other endeavors and indulge this craving to the detriment of familial and social attachments, naturally should not entertain retiring if at all possible. These people usually have few pursuits outside of work and many would find the retired state wasteful and unfulfilling.

Adaptability is a prerequisite character trait which can foretell how an individual will ease into retirement mode. People who have had different careers during their employment lifetimes, adjusting adequately to each change of venue, can usually be counted on to move on from one phase of life to another without great difficulty.

Hysteroid and depressive individuals, who tend to exhibit extreme emotional responses to life's changes, no matter what they might be, usually find retirement challenging. However, on occasion, relief from the stress of the need to perform at an expected level might even prove therapeutic.

REGIMENTATION

One of the most difficult tasks of adaptation to a retired state is overcoming the years of adherence to a pattern of behavior. Whether we are aware of it or not, responses to the stress of environmental stimuli become routine, and coupled with the added pressures of the workplace can cause subliminal or overt anxiety reactions. This is why we look forward to weekends and vacations, to get away from the cause of this discomfort. Over time these responses become an integral part of our makeup. At the extreme, some people always seem edgy, easily riled, even argumentative with or without any obvious cause. Some continually feel under some sort of pressure, with the need to conquer an ever-existing challenge.

A successful retirement should serve as a perpetual vacation, a time to unwind from the regimentation of a former career and the anxieties of the past. It should be a time when the worries of younger years seem trivial and are put to rest, a time for healing the wounds of the spirit.

NEGATIVITY

Let's explore two extremes in the workplace. The first is the outsider, who by personality or desire doesn't fit in or shows no drive to progress in his job, perhaps getting little or no pleasure out of the work, one who feels cast out or even a victim of the bullying that unfortunately exists in many industries, the "office dupe" who is the butt of jokes. The other extreme is the attempted overachiever, the "lab rat" or "brown noser," who is often abused by pranks. For these individuals, no matter how motivated or dedicated they may be, work can be a living hell, because the negativity from fellow employees is felt as a daily punishment. To these men and women, absence from work can be seen as a blessing, a reprieve from the grind of employment.

CULTURE

Work has been glorified as a gratifying endeavor in the western world; however, in some other countries leisure has assumed much greater prominence. When one has been brought up to aspire to a certain goal, the attempt to achieve that goal is then accredited to be the highest aspiration. You work to live, but you live to luxuriate, to love, to enjoy, to pursue and experience happiness. Therefore, while you can achieve through useful endeavor, you can exhilarate and perhaps gain a greater sense of peace and serenity with a successful retirement. Under such circumstances, the retreat of a religious monk to pray and to meditate could be considered a form of retirement.

ORIENTATION

Sometimes I feel as though I must be a naturally lazy person to enjoy being retired as much as I do. Then I remind myself of the half century of continuous professional work I put in, often being involved in several different areas of endeavor at the same time. Early on I worked many hours, sixty or seventy each week. My wife sometimes kept my daughter up past midnight when she was still a toddler so I could have time to play with her. My wife feared that otherwise my daughter would not truly know her father. I feel that she was such a great mother, she more than made up for any deficiency on my part. My daughter says that we both were great parents and that's all that really matters.

I often wonder if the milieu I grew up in had something to do with how easily I have gone from a busy work schedule to retirement. I grew up poor, the son of immigrant parents. We lived in what is now called the Bedford-Stuyvesant section of Brooklyn, New York, in a transitional period for that neighborhood. I had many bright friends, who at a young age discussed worldly matters in quite an adult fashion. Today young people choose professional athletes or movie stars as their idols. We most envied the European nobility who didn't have to work, living in luxury without monetary worries. Listening to our parents complain about hardships of the working poor—long hours and low wages—obviously had an impact.

Being indoctrinated, at a young age, into a culture of living frugally because of need, orientation or desire during the Great Depression and fearing the next economic downturn had a great influence on the decisions I have made in steering a conservative course in my life. It is reasonable to deduce that I have been guided unconsciously to emulate the lifestyle of the idle nobility I romanticized as a child.

SECURITY

It can be frightening to voluntarily walk away from a good job that is challenging and entertaining to begin an uncertain, relatively idle future. However, it is not as devastating as having to acutely adjust to an unemployed state due to corporate downsizing or an unforeseen bankruptcy. In either case, proper preparation can mitigate the trauma.

Longtime employment in one location can create a sense of security, belonging and trust. When this trust is broken, the harsh realization that each individual employee is ultimately on his or her own leads to the detriment of the sense of security. It is therefore important that each worker, whether low-level employee, self-employed, middle management or executive, understands that the comfort of their future and the comfort of their family is their sole responsibility. From the first day of eligibility, the worker should become knowledgeable about the pension benefits due him or her. Like the security all federal government workers have in knowing that a pension awaits them when they retire, all non-government workers should keep informed about the safety and availability of the benefits they can count on after they retire and the dollar amount they are due. If a union is involved, a representative should be sought out for clarification of the details. Many workers have chosen lower-paying positions with better benefits over higher-paying jobs with lesser benefits.

Even in more secure situations, where there are adequate funds available, the uncertainty of market fluctuations, with severe downturns an ever-present danger, the decision to give up earning and to depend solely on investments can be a difficult one to make.

HEALTH

The state of one's health is always a factor in determining if and when one should retire. Robust individuals, constantly reassured by comforting medical check-ups, often assume they are just as hardy as they were years before and feel they can take on a workload equal to or even beyond the capabilities of younger, less experienced competitors. Sometimes this is foolish and leads to dire consequences, but on many occasions this proves to be a true assessment of one's vitality and ability. No one who can fully carry out his duties, loves what he does, is good at it and gains satisfaction in the adequate completion of the tasks laid before him should consider voluntarily retiring unless forced to do so by factors not under his control. One of those important factors is failing health.

Ranking among the most common medical problems interfering with productivity, cardiac disease can be, in its most severe form, life threatening. The initial symptoms, such as anginal chest pain, should always be regarded as a wake-up call to let a person know it is time to slow down, reduce working responsibilities, or even consider quitting work altogether if possible. In many cases the condition may remain a minor one and no major changes would then be necessary; however, constant vigilance should be exercised to detect a worsening of symptoms and the need for further stress reduction. With the latest cardiac surgical procedures, such as bypass and stent emplacement, many workers may return to a reasonable facsimile of their previous schedule after a short recovery period. Those who cannot should be considered to be candidates for retirement.

Although patients with longstanding, especially terminal, illness are usually dismissed from work on medical leave, some self-employed individuals may find distraction from the unpleasantness of their affliction and side effects from therapy by continuing to perform whatever duties of their cherished occupation they still can. The rest should be afforded a well-deserved retirement.

STATUS AND RESPONSIBILITY

I have known people who wanted to retire, could afford to retire, but due to their status or responsibility could not. One, a successful businessman, could not find a suitable buyer for the company he started and since he was not expendable, due to a unique artistic talent he possessed, he could not find a replacement for himself. Not wishing to dissolve his company and feeling responsible for the welfare of his employees, he continued to go to work each day until he died. He wanted very much to retire to a carefree life, but morally he could not live with the knowledge that he would put two hundred people out of work.

In some families, after the children have been raised, educated and have left home to live separate lives, the burden of caring for older parents falls on the "in-between" generation, often interfering with retirement plans. Even if they don't live in the same house, although that would be an obvious diversion, the need to be close by and on call for any of a myriad of geriatric emergencies would interfere with any desire to relocate. If the parent or parents are financially dependent, the cost burden might be just enough to derail any retirement plans until the death of all those dependents.

LIFESTYLE

The very affluent do not have to be concerned with downsizing after retirement, but the majority of retirees may find that they do have to curtail their lifestyles in relation to the success or failure of their financial planning. Hopefully those who adhere to the formulas outlined in this book and start at a young enough age will avoid the need to cut back on their reasonable expectations. Most projections of the financial needs of retired families anticipate that most, if not all, liabilities, such as mortgages and other loans have been satisfied. Retiring with large debts not covered by substantial assets is not advised.

The question must be asked if a family could be comfortable giving up some of the everyday luxuries they have become accustomed to and still function acceptably. Which ones? How much has to be sliced from the family budget? How should spending be curtailed? Should shopping sprees be eliminated? Should we move to a smaller home or buy a less expensive car?

To some individuals the status of being able to spend freely and accumulate "stuff" is very important in the evaluation of self-worth. What you have is equated to who you are. It is seen as the measure of your success. Throughout history, one has been evaluated by one's possessions, whether it be the number of servants, cattle, homes, acreage of land or money. Today many people find this to be shallow thinking, but others discover it is very difficult to retire to a standard of living below what has become their norm in past years.

The family members involved in households with limited means must get together and decide whether they could be comfortable existing under the restraints of a lower standard of living or would an alternate course other than retirement be more advisable, if that option is available.

HOBBIES

Since childhood I have been attracted to the sea. When I was young, I used a tree branch for a fishing rod to fish off a pier and loved to go to the beach and swim. Now, in retirement, I answer the soothing call of the sea. As I sit in front of my computer,

I often glance out the window at the lagoon that serves as my muse. Deep sea fishing is my passion. I never feel closer to nature, or God if you are so inclined, than when I toil in my garden or when I am out at sea. The sea calms me better than any chemical tranquilizer ever could. The thrill of hooking and reeling in a fish after a sporting battle refreshes my spirit. It is a spiritual exercise. The sea is my temple, my escape from the world. When the weather doesn't allow outside activities and I'm not writing, I paint. Many of the walls in my house are now adorned with my best efforts.

Like many jobs, the work that I did for over forty years—listening to people hour upon hour of each working day talking about their deepest thoughts and darkest secrets, requesting help with difficult aspects of their lives and relief from troubling symptoms—was stressful. Although I enjoyed the work immensely and described it like being involved in an interactive soap opera on television all day long, after several months of this heavy burden of responsibility I literally demanded a vacation. These were not vacations of choice, but of necessity, to refresh myself so I could continue functioning at the level required to be at peace and helpful to my patients.

Now that I no longer treat disturbed people, many of whom exhibited vile and unpleasant symptomatology, vacations are once again a luxury and not a necessity. Since my wife and I now enjoy perpetual vacation time, long periods away are no longer needed. Shorter breaks in the usual routine suffice to serve as restoring escapes from the business of everyday living.

Involvement in our hobbies gives us adequate time away from chores to experience such periods of escape from the ordinary.

Reading a good book, riding a bicycle, playing a pleasurable sport or enjoying a lovely day at sea can be adequate vacation substitutes during retirement years, especially when age and physicality curtail maneuverability and make travel a bother.

I want to make a strong case for gardening as a hobby. Some men may consider this a less masculine endeavor, but let me tell you, there are few better ways to exercise and appreciate nature than by planting flowers, pruning shrubs or pulling weeds. Without realizing it, in a few hours you have done hundreds of deep knee bends. Planting or chopping down a tree can give your biceps and triceps a workout. However, the true glory is in the communion with nature: making and watching things grow, giving birth to living things. Thirty-five years ago I planted twenty-six evergreen trees, two rows of thirteen on each side of our small plot of ground. Some of these trees have risen to nearly thirty feet high, giving us much-desired privacy, as houses in shore communities such as ours tend to be built close together. Whenever I look at the rows of greenery at our property edges I appreciate their beauty with a sense of pride.

FRUGALITY

My love for the sea initiated my great wish to live on a large boat and travel at my pleasure. While this was still a pipedream, my wife and I enjoyed taking sea cruises with friends and family during vacation times. When the dream became more of a quest, we began to charter yachts with two other couples to experience life on the sea. What I discovered was a revelation. Buying a live-aboard boat not only entails the initial purchase cost, but the upkeep may be quite expensive. If the owner cannot afford a captain and a crew then he has to become an expert mechanic to tend to the engines by himself while away from shore. However, the more I learned about the costs and difficulties of being the owner of a relatively large boat, the more I realized that I could not afford it and, even if I could, it would at best be a temporary way of life of which we would ultimately tire. We would then hope we could sell our boat for a sufficient fraction of the original cost to be able to buy a new house. So we stayed in our old house, to keep my dream from becoming a nightmare.

Many people do stray into nightmarish situations by allowing their fantasies to overrule their good common sense. God knows what difficulties I would have run into if I had thrown caution to the wind and proceeded to spend my savings on a vessel I could ill afford. I probably would never have made it to retirement and would not be writing this book now. Whatever pleasure I would have experienced might have been drowned in the difficulties encountered out on the open sea.

Each year many new entrepreneurs go bankrupt. Thousands of workers who dream of being self-employed leave their jobs and go out on their own. Those who are fully prepared and perform adequate due diligence have a chance for success. Others, who through lack of education or preparation or both begin either under-capitalized or over-capitalized, are usually doomed to fail. Having a dream is a good thing, if it's a possible dream. As with Don Quixote, impossible dreams lead to failure. Depending on the age of the individual or the amount of the loss, a business failure can obliterate the dream of any retirement.

Appreciate the value of frugality in choosing a lifestyle, if retirement is a goal when one no longer works at a daily job. More wild schemes are prone to fail than to succeed. At a young age one can fail and try again, because time is not yet a major factor, but at an advanced age time is precious.

BURNOUT

As I brought up earlier, the greatest determinant in regard to retirement readiness is self-awareness. The recognition of when one has reached his or her limit with a vocation is vital to knowing when it is time to quit and move on.

In my own life I have had several such epiphanies. As an undergraduate I trained to be a pharmacist, but after several years behind pharmacy counters I realized I would never be satisfied filling out prescriptions ordered by others. I wanted to be the physician making the diagnosis and writing the prescriptions. I wanted the responsibility of issuing the orders for the care and therapy of the patient. I consider pharmacy a noble profession and cherish it for having given me the ability to work and earn enough to pay my medical school tuition fees. However, I wanted to go on to study medicine.

Later I had a career choice to make. Throughout my medical school training I had envisioned myself becoming an internist and was sure it was my future to practice internal medicine, so I declined a prized surgical residency with the assurance of a partnership in a lucrative practice. However, during my internship I reassessed myself, my desires and abilities and determined I was best suited to the practice of psychiatry.

Upon completing my psychiatric residency, I was offered junior partnerships in the practices of two of the busiest psychiatrists in Philadelphia, Pennsylvania. Although this would mean less start-up costs, with shared expenses, I declined these invitations. I knew I would find the greatest gratification in building my own practice and doing it my way. So, despite having meager savings, I went out on my own.

For twenty-five years I lectured as a professor of psychiatry at a medical school and was invited to lecture at prominent universities. I became a leading candidate to become the chairman of my department, the position I had been groomed for by the retiring chairman. After careful soul searching I determined I was not cut out for the politics of academia. Soon I left both my clinical and lecturing activities at the medical college to devote myself wholly to my private practice, a decision I have never regretted.

My care of patients, both in office psychotherapy sessions and inpatient settings at hospitals and geriatric centers, became my prime concern and my great pleasure and honor of service. Teaching is a meaningful endeavor and I am indebted for the opportunity I was afforded, but attempting to heal and mitigate pain and suffering was my true calling.

After a number of years, like many practitioners who find the business of their profession overwhelming the desired aspects of their labors, with less time to devote to the work they love and more needed for administration, I began to tire of the interference of insurance companies and the loss of patient confidentiality. When insurance officials' meddling began to deny adequate patient care, I knew it was time to call it quits.

I was unable to adapt to the new way of doing things: placing the best care of a patient secondary to the whim of an insurance decision. This is not what I signed up for. I grew weary of the pressure placed on me by officials to cut corners in administering care. So I severed my relations with those who caved in to the rationers of care and reached deep within myself and realized I was burned out. What I loved dearly had been taken from me and it could not be regained, so I decided that after fifty years of being involved with the delivery of health care, it was time to retire.

ADJUSTMENT

In all honesty, if I couldn't financially afford to retire at the time I did, because I no longer could abide by the rules that were forcing me to compromise my integrity, I would have had to adjust to doing things against my conscience. How many of you readers have to do just that? Having to comply with commands from supervisors that you know are just not right, or even absolutely wrong, to make some deadline, meet a quota or keep within budget? That is why it is so important that you are financially secure later in life so that you cannot be bullied into sacrificing your integrity for a paycheck. Money cannot buy happiness and only in a pet store can it buy love, but it surely can give you a sense of freedom and independence.

The thought of having to compromise my principles to appease some official of an insurance company making a huge salary while patients are being deprived of adequate care raised my ire. If I had to do things that way I knew I would have trouble sleeping at night.

PASSION

It's easy to sense the passion in the words I use to express the vehemence I feel toward those who forced me to leave a practice I adored. You see, I never wanted to stop working at my labor of love. Fortunately, I had planned for retirement in case it became a necessity, but I never really expected it to happen. I feel as though I was forced out; it's as if I were fired from my job. Therefore, I can relate to anyone who has actually been fired against his will. I was given a type of a pink slip too. I know how it feels. I can commiserate.

When you have devoted yourself to a cause or a company for many years as I had and suddenly find out that you no longer belong, through no fault of your own but because they changed the rules, it's painful to realize the game is being played at a lower level. There I was, in my clinical prime and fueled by years of experience, forced to retire because I wouldn't lower my standards. I hope that all of you out there who want to excel at what you do, if you are called upon to compromise your integrity, have gained the wherewithal and the courage to thumb your noses at mediocrity.

IMPORTANCE

Respect what you do. An honest job, no matter how menial, fulfills a purpose. However, if you don't feel your work is important to you, you are in the wrong line of work, no matter how glamorous it may seem to others.

Many years ago I was discovered to have a fine tenor voice and offered a scholarship to train with a famous vocal coach. I sang for a number of years at his studio and he obtained some roles for me in local productions, until it came time for me to make a career choice. Did I wish to make a career in music or pursue a life in health care? Among the most important factors which swayed my decision was my need to feel the importance of my work. I wanted to do something that mattered. Finally, I decided that to help others in their time of need and disability was more important, in my estimation, than entertaining an audience with song. Feeling important to yourself is crucial. It makes you feel as though you count. You are a contributor, a useful member of society.

Losing the work that is important to you, especially when it is ripped from you through no fault of your own, because of some ill-advised decision of a superior, change of company policy or government miscalculation, can be agonizing and demoralizing if you have no backup plan. Possess a retirement backup plan, especially if you have reached middle years.

EXPENSES

You must always know the extent of your expenditures, yet many people have no idea of what their budgetary limitations are. Only when they max out their credit cards do they appreciate the amount of their debts. Bankruptcy is a credit wrecker and should be avoided at all costs, if retirement is in future plans. Some resilient souls may overcome a bankruptcy with a strategic comeback, but the interim phase is usually painful and best to be avoided. Try the best you can to know where every penny goes, so you can know when you can truly afford whatever luxurious items you may wish to purchase. Always keep your assets and liabilities in balance. Run your household so that all necessities are paid for first before budgeting for other items. Save today so you can spend another day.

SAVING

Although the formulas for timely saving and investing for specific situations, time periods and retirement needs will be addressed in great detail in the next part of this book, let's discuss some basic fundamentals now.

It is important to indoctrinate each child into the habit of saving. At a young age, perhaps in the first or second grade of elementary school, the parent should physically take the child to the bank and open a savings or money market account in joint ownership, so the child can appreciate having money set aside in his or her own name. Over the years such an account can be added to and earmarked for specific purposes, such as school tuition, birthday parties, weddings or the like. In periods of low interest rates, as soon as feasible, this account can be augmented with higher-interest-bearing investments, always bearing in mind that the non-bank investments do not carry the guarantee of the federal government and therefore are more risky.

One should always be wary of placing assets in a trust for minors, for specific purposes, into investments bearing high risks. Even the best of stocks fall in a down market and, when that money is needed, you may find it necessary to sell at a loss. After suffering a severe financial setback of his own, Mark Twain said, "It's not the return on your money that you should be concerned about, it's the return of your money." High-risk investments can lead to sizeable, or even total, loss of capital. Always remember you should begin to invest only after you have accumulated sufficient capital in interest-bearing government-secured accounts.

When asked what was the most wonderful equation he had ever encountered, Albert Einstein answered "compound interest." No matter how meager that interest might be, in a guaranteed account the money is not only safe, but it is also growing. I will never forget accompanying my mother when I was still very little as we trekked many city blocks to a savings bank. There were commercial banks closer to where we lived, but the savings bank offered one percent higher interest. She explained to me that the one percent difference meant we could afford another new pair of shoes although money was very tight that year.

Teaching a child to save at a young age will instill a sense of fiscal responsibility that can last a lifetime. This disciplined approach to saving and later investing for the future is the backbone of the planning strategy for a financially-secure retirement. The infant is never too young to start to learn a language and the child is never too young to learn the value of money.

SAFETY

Just as I stress safety in investing, general safety must also be a concern in choosing when it is the proper time to consider retirement. Most public employees already have age and physical capability guidelines in place in those jobs where employee safety is involved. Many private sectors, where there is danger in the workplace for aging employees, enforce mandatory retirement rules. It is those positions where individual decisions about retirement are the usual course that common sense has to trump stubborn pride. A younger medical director or department chief has to tell an older surgeon when it's time to put down his scalpel for the last time, for his own good and his patients' well-being. Often this is a committee decision, but when the aging surgeon is a respected professional and has in the past mentored those who are judging him, this can lead to a difficult confrontation.

Whenever failing physical skills are a factor in compromising safety and the individual doesn't seem to be aware of this happening or chooses to ignore the consequences of continuing to perform, it is beneficial for someone with authority to step in and inform the individual the time to retire has come.

STRESS

Although many occupations are stressful, resourceful workers find ways to handle the day-to-day aggravation that goes with their jobs. However, the grief factor can build up until it becomes difficult and then impossible to handle. Because only that individual feels the stress, he or she is the only one who can assess when it has become intolerable.

Stress is the cause of many lost work days due to absences each year. It should be the duty of every responsible supervisor to limit any harassment or intimidation that occurs in the workplace. The place of employment should be kept as free of any controllable stressful situation as possible. Factors such as meeting deadlines, coming in below budget or fighting against the odds to keep people alive are stressful enough; augment them with the torment of cruel coworkers and the stress can become intolerable and cause premature retirement.

TIME OF LIFE

As one grows older, the ability to adjust to the negative aspects of life gets harder. A mere bump or bruise tends to hurt more and heal slower. Pain becomes a constant companion and little slights are not taken as lightly. The aging individual is more easily riled and apt to be grumpy. Chronic pain does that. As eyesight dims and hearing grows less acute, the person tends to speak louder and get more readily annoyed. It's the price you pay for having survived. Aging men and women tend to be insulted when corrected or disregarded by younger ones they feel should be paying them more respect. Fewer things excite older people. Fewer pure pleasures draw their attention. Things that were once thought to be indispensable no longer seem so.

For many, work is truly a blessing, a necessity of life. For the man or woman who started a small business and watched it grow, perhaps hiring family members or friends, the business may be loved like a child, something nurtured and cared for. When this much importance is attached to an endeavor and infirmity does not interfere with carrying out the usual work of the position, if you enjoy what you do and you are your own boss, why think of retiring before you no longer can do the job?

For men and women who have this familial attachment to their work, leaving it or even diminishing their responsibilities could prove quite detrimental in some cases. Those who live to work and truly love to go to work each day should continue until they no longer can. I was once like that.

I truly loved what I did and never dreamt I would retire, until the nature of the work changed and all the fulfillment was gone. So I truly understand the hardship in leaving the work you love, even to embark on a challenging new road of life.

FAMILY

Retirement of one or both of the principal wage earners affects all the family members and should be treated as a family affair. Careful planning and preparation for future living arrangements, budgetary restraints and other essential elements of life changes should be fully discussed before the fact, so it is clear to your partner and family what the future situation will be. It is best to have a family meeting, even if it's just two people, so no misunderstandings occur later on about what the new responsibilities will be.

When just one of the main earners retires, while the other one remains employed, the family dynamics still may alter greatly. Domestic duties and responsibilities may have to shift from the wage earner to the retiree. This is more commonly seen in traditional unions when the male retires while the female remains working. Food shopping and even cooking, depending on the skill of the individual, as well as housekeeping, may now increasingly become the duty of the retired one.

The change of main wage earner may be a period of stressful adjustment. It is best for such feelings to be anticipated and hashed out beforehand to avoid dissension later. After the children have left home, a situation hoped for before the retirement of the parents, money matters can become the most frequent cause for argument between retired couples.

In difficult economies, when jobs are hard to find, many grown single people are forced to live with their parents. For many reasons this places unexpected pressure on any retirement relationship. When the parents' home can physically accommodate more than one person, either an additional sibling or a spouse, this can become a detriment to retirement plans. Many good parents have been known to have had to defer retiring to care for dependent children and that is why financial planning should prepare for providing the funds to accommodate such eventualities.

Parenthood brings on vast responsibilities. One, definitely, is to provide for the welfare of the child. In less fortunate homes, some children never leave. Because of illness or disability, these children have to be cared for from the cradle to the grave. If they are to receive care after their parents die, adequate funds have to be put aside beforehand. Such financial requirements may delay or even abrogate retirement, even in otherwise affluent households.

There are many actions that family members can take to enhance or deter retirement plans, ranging from retirement parties and generous gifts to fighting over the inheritance. Some families are wonderful examples of how life should be lived, while others reek with envy and belligerence. Like with most things, people get out of their relationships what they put into them. So be good to your kids—they just might be the ones who choose how comfortable your nursing home is. From personal experience I can tell you that some nursing homes are pretty bad places to spend your last days.

People who come from homes filled with strife and hostility are disadvantaged when starting families of their own, because they lack the memory of positive examples to emulate. An old saying imparts, "If you want to have a happy marriage, marry someone who comes from a happy marriage." With over 50 percent of marriages ending in divorce and many couples today choosing cohabitation over traditional unions, many people unfortunately are not the products of happy marriages. However, children should never be the victims of the failure of their parents and their welfare should not be sacrificed to satisfy the selfishness of someone who caused them to be. Adequate funds should always be made available for their needs.

OCCUPATION

Some jobs you never want to leave and others you can't wait to get away from. Also, there are jobs you might not want to leave, but you just can't go on doing them due to physical limitations or other problems.

Certain occupations allow you to continue working until the day you die. You can sit behind your desk in an office, perusing papers or talking on the telephone, till you grow senile or keel over. Weather-related, physically demanding labor such as construction work carries an expiration date. If you haven't progressed upstairs to a desk job, your employment years are numbered. Theoretically a psychiatrist, who spends most of his or her time seated, can work until his hearing goes, while a surgeon, who works on his or her feet and requires manual dexterity, is required to quit when he or she can no longer perform physically.

Different occupations have different anticipated longevity. The length of time you can work your chosen career dictates the intensity of your preparation for retirement. If you can only toil twenty years at a strenuous job, with an insufficient pension, you can't begin to save for retirement after fifteen years on the job. You must begin much earlier or plan for a second career that is easier for you to handle.

Projections of years to be working, salary increases, bonuses, job security, pension benefit accumulation, carrying benefits over from one job to another and length of periods of unemployment in between jobs all figure prominently in planning for an adequate retirement early enough so that the reasonable dreams of a lifetime can be fulfilled in retirement.

SALARY

How much you make, in some cases, is not as important as how much you have accumulated in retirement accounts, in regard to preparation for retirement. If you earn one million dollars a year, spend nine hundred and fifty thousand and invest only fifty thousand, over a period of time you may not be as financially secure as someone else who earns three hundred thousand dollars per year and frugally invests one hundred thousand. The millionaire cited would have to have investments that appreciate at a much greater rate than the more conservative investor just to be able to afford a retirement lifestyle on the same level as the frugal one, who earns less than one-third the salary.

Recent studies have shown that many professional athletes who make large salaries are broke just a few years after no longer being able to play their sport. The same is true of lottery winners who sometimes suffer the same fate. Usually coming from humble backgrounds, with little financial sophistication, they are overwhelmed by their good luck and are prone to overindulge in fulfilling their childhood wishes and desires. They tend to spend on items which do not have lasting value and depreciate rapidly. They do not appreciate the necessity of the future need for money. When money comes easily, just like with most things, it is not as respected as when it is earned through hard labor and is readily squandered. In their newfound celebrity, they equate status with generosity and become easy prey for family and friends who wish to exploit that generosity. The atmosphere around them is laden with the call to share the bonanza, that it is the duty of the winner to reimburse all who had some relation to the winner. In the extreme, an entourage of parasites forms about them, reminding them of humble beginnings and that it is their responsibility to give back to their old buddies. Old acquaintances become new close friends until the money runs out and then they become distant again.

Retirement saving is a modern-day necessity in an age where Social Security benefits are insufficient to sustain a lifestyle to which most people are accustomed and the very future of the fund's availability is constantly a media question. To squander newfound wealth on trinkets and adornments and erstwhile companions, while neglecting to attend to the needs of the future, is a road to financial disaster. Conversely, affordable charitable work guided by responsible managers, which can benefit depressed communities, is quite commendable.

It has long been recognized that great wealth brings great responsibility; but this is beyond the understanding of ordinary people who may try to emulate what the super-rich do. It has been written that the rich are different. They don't need my advice on retirement; they have adequate advisers of their own and I'm not writing for them. However, for a young person who is fortunate enough to have a lucrative contract, to have come into a sizeable inheritance or who has won big at a game of chance, to undertake vast financial obligations to boost status and self-esteem is unwise.

One of the first professional golfers, Walter Hagen, said, "I don't want to be a millionaire; I just want to live like one."[2] It is quite understandable that we all would like to live in mansions, with servants catering to our every whim, be driven by chauffeurs in limousines, have yachts and private planes with pilots flying us to exotic vacation locales. There's nothing wrong with such desires if you can afford them. In the United States as well as some other countries, with easy credit available, living beyond one's means has become the norm rather than the exception.

Families overspend on all sorts of frivolous items, neglecting the necessities of the future. If all the money spent on toys and games and unneeded products, readily outgrown, would be placed instead in college funds, maybe students would have less debt when they graduate and go into the job market. Student debt has exploded as parents can no longer carry the burden of college tuition, while sales of music albums and other luxurious items have made many singers very wealthy. The excuse of needed frivolities to complete a childhood at the expense of needed planning for the future have left many students starting out with tremendous financial obligations before they have earned one cent. People place emphasis on the unimportant and, in many cases, neglect what is important.

Since America has the most stable financial system, with no history of default, countries around the world feel secure buying our debt. So, some people keep going further and further into debt; depending on our children and children's children to pay off the interest on treasury notes and bonds as they come due. Many economists continue to remind us of the frightening condition that our future and security is actually mortgaged and, should we ever lose the position of our currency being the standard of the world, which China and other countries are pushing for, we would be in grave trouble.

Unlike the government, the average American family can't print its own currency and can't delay paying off its debts in perpetuity. We have to learn to live within our means and not be guided by the envy we have of the lifestyles we see on television and in motion pictures. Children have to be taught from the crib that certain things are affordable and others are not. Just as we teach our children physical discipline, they have to be instilled with financial discipline at an early age.

An overwhelming number of middle-class farmers, merchants and professionals would like to know they can look forward to a comfortable retirement in their advanced years. For this to occur, it is mandatory that the importance of financial discipline be understood. Most middle-income families today do not have sufficient money put aside to fund an acceptable retirement. It is a national embarrassment. As noted before, this is a family's responsibility. It should be taught from early childhood, just like the mathematics needed to discern that the numbers are right to undertake retirement. We must impart this critical knowledge to our children, as part of their inheritance, so that they will have an easier life than we did.

WEIGHING THE PROS AND CONS

When termination of employment occurs beyond the choice of the individual, then one must weigh the pros and cons of retirement carefully. Is one psychologically ready to retire or not? Can one afford to retire or not? Is retirement even a logical solution to all the problems associated with the loss of work and earning abilities? Does the individual have sufficient outside interests to sustain a contented retirement, which may last many years, depending on the age of the retiree and life expectancy? When such a dismissal from work comes abruptly, without a suitable adjustment period and with little or no time to make adequate plans, the initial post-work period can be traumatic and sobering.

Even if retirement is still a viable option, this may be a period of frenzy and critical reevaluation, a time to recalculate the needs and potential of the future, a time to take stock of yourself and your assets and liabilities, a time to learn who you really are.

Are you cut out for a life of leisure and relaxation or have you become so enamored with the regimentation of the work routine, to the dismissal of most else, that you would be lost without it? You have to take the time to learn to know yourself as never before, to know who you really are and what your true desires are, because you are making one of the great decisions of life. It may rank along with your choice of what occupation to enter into and whom to marry.

Even if retirement is a free choice, with adequate time to prepare and all contingencies accounted for, it is a major step—a life-altering decision, which should be treated like one. It means a change of routine, perhaps a change of living arrangements, moving to a new location, making new friends and leaving old ones. Nurturing factors of the living environment, such as doctors, hospitals, religious and educational centers, might have to change. If a spiritual adviser has become a source of comfort, a new one may have to be found. In some cases, the new venue of existence may represent a radical departure from the old and require a period of adjustment, perhaps even a difficult one.

All these factors must be taken into account, as well as the need for agreement on the part of all involved. In a spousal arrangement, it is very important that both partners are ready to assume the new lifestyle and to make whatever sacrifices are required to make it work. As in much of life, what you get out of retirement has a lot to do with what you put in. If one enters into what may be the end phase of life with enthusiasm and love, one can expect to reap a harvest of joy and happiness.

CHAPTER 3

Your Retirement Environment

Successful retirees are good citizens. They are self-sufficient and aid the economy by leaving the workforce at an appropriate time, to allow someone else with comparable work skills to move into their jobs. By doing so, down the line, they may even facilitate the hiring of a previously unemployed person into an entry-level position. If all eligible workers were able to retire comfortably at the earliest acceptable age, many younger and lower-waged workers could then enter the workforce. Many companies have recognized the advantage of such a policy and have offered early retirement packages, some quite generous, recognizing that in time this would prove cost-effective.

This is not to be misunderstood. I am not advocating a mass layoff of higher-paid, skilled veteran employees to make room for cheaper labor. However, technological advancements have made unemployment a problem for many nations and the creation of opportunities for new workers is of paramount importance.

Many jobs have become obsolete. People are being replaced by machines. Robots help make automobiles and the city of Detroit has filed for bankruptcy. Robots don't shop, spend money or pay taxes. They don't contribute to the economy the way people do.

The creation of jobs is a prime concern of government economic planners. It is vital for our economy.

ECONOMY

America is a capitalistic society. Unlike socialistic societies where nearly everyone works for the government, in our free enterprise system independent businesses are relied upon to supply jobs for much of the workforce.

Small businesses usually grow much faster than large established ones and therefore hire a sizeable number of new employees. The hiring of new employees is usually a sign of company growth and prosperity and, since upper management is usually rewarded in line with the growth of company profit and increase in share price, in the business world a person's financial worth may be measured by how many new jobs he or she caused to be created. Chief executive officers of corporations are counted among the highest-salaried men and women in the land.

CONSUMERS

Two-thirds of the gross national product of the United States is dependent upon the American consumer. As we currently import much more than we export, we support foreign economies as well. Since we have the highest standard of living of all the large countries, the spending of the American family is therefore the financial backbone of the world. American families, emulating their government, are going into debt to satisfy their desire to accumulate goods and services.

Unfortunately, this craving to satisfy our need for things interferes with our ability to save. Seeing lifestyles way above what we can afford in motion pictures and on television makes us want to live richly even when we are not rich. We don't want to seem like failures to our children, so we indulge their pleas for games and toys beyond our means. We have the need to spend to impress others. Many people have taken this to an extreme and the number of personal bankruptcies has increased.

This lack of fiscal discipline has left the majority of American workers with inadequate funds in their retirement accounts to support a comfortable retirement. Most people are going to depend on Social Security checks and meager, or even unreliable, company pension plan payments. Poor planning, late planning, premature borrowing, depleting of retirement accounts and reckless spending can cause the retirement years to be both difficult and uncomfortable. Squandering potential retirement funds, so that the retiree is more dependent on government facilities, exacerbates the national debt.

SOCIAL SECURITY

Although we are constantly hearing and reading about the difficulties that the United States' Social Security system is projected to have in the future due to unwise government decisions, it is politically unthinkable that payments will be significantly interfered with any time soon. What may be reduced, however, are the cost-of-living increases. This reduction in anticipated income during periods of increasing inflation, considering the continuous increase in Medicare costs, should be factored into tight budgets and retirement investment planning.

At any rate, Social Security alone will barely take most folks out of the poverty level and these payments should only be used as a base to build upon with other investments, for any kind of comfort level in retirement.

ECONOMICS

Governmental relationships to the governed have been guided by two differing Chinese philosophies over the past twenty-five hundred years.

Confucius taught that rulers should be wise and set a positive example for their subjects, caring for their needs in a paternalistic fashion.[3]

Lao Tsu criticized Confucius for advocating a major role for government in the lives of its citizens. Lao Tsu taught that the proper way was to stand aside from the leadership and provide for the needs of life by oneself.[4]

From the events of the past century, we have learned that the most effective approach is to incorporate elements of both philosophies. Governments must have agencies to aid the indigent and the disabled, to care for infrastructure and the environment, while the paternalistic "cradle to the grave" benefits of socialistic countries have led to economic ruin. This lesson has to be applied to individual preparation for retirement.

During periods of recession, companies fail. Retirement benefits may be lost. Local government pensions may be restructured. Contracts may be altered. Although Social Security benefits are a guaranteed annuity-like payment, the provisions of the law can be modified. These outside benefits, once thought to be inviolate, are no longer totally reliable to yield the amount counted on to be available when needed to sustain desirable family expenditures. Therefore, all people who are able need to realize the wisdom of a plan to accumulate sufficient assets in their own accounts to augment outside funds in the amounts required to allow living the life envisioned after the working years are over.

The earlier in life the plan for retirement is put in place, the easier it will be to achieve the desired goals. It is never too early to start saving for retirement. I wish I had heeded the advice of my first insurance agent. When I went into practice he implored me to invest fifty dollars each week in a mutual fund. The ghostly specter of men on Wall Street jumping out of windows during the stock market crash of the late 1920s haunted America and many were advising me to stay away from the stock market. So I didn't start investing until much later. The Dow Jones Industrial Average was at 500 then. In February 2014, the Dow Jones Industrial average was over 15,000 points higher, an increase of over 3000 percent. I should have listened to the sage advice of an older man, himself a wise investor. I hope many of you readers will be wiser and braver than I was as a young professional just embarking on my career and start to save and invest at as early an age as possible.

DEBT

Any retirement funding plan must assume the retiree is major debt-free. Only if you have substantially more coming to you in investment income than you require to cover your usual expenses should you be holding large debts. If the average middle-income family still owes on a sizeable mortgage, they are not adequately prepared for retirement. That is why many financial advisers will tell you to pay off your mortgage as soon as you can.

Do not be guided in your investment decisions solely by the tax advantages. The psychological comfort in knowing that you own your own home, free and clear, come what may, overcomes any taxes saved with mortgage deductions. The most devastating event that can befall a family is having to leave their home because of job loss or other financial catastrophe and inability to meet mortgage payments. Although many banks will renegotiate more manageable rates during difficult times, when no payments are possible to be made over a reasonable time, the family will have to vacate their home. Always be prepared against the eventuality of an unforeseen disaster.

INSURANCE

Many homes in the northeastern part of the United States were destroyed or severely damaged by Superstorm Sandy in 2012. Many had not been repaired or restored even two years later. The havoc and devastation caused by this hurricane were immense. Most of the damage was done by flooding. Homeowners who had only government-supplied flood insurance were dismayed to learn how little it covered. Those who were wise enough to realize how little reimbursement the government insurance afforded and purchased extra flood insurance through private companies made out much better. Homes and businesses which had insufficient coverage had to beseech their governors for additional funds to rebuild. These public funds have so far been slow in coming. Even when private insurance companies have been lax in making payments, because of the gravity of their losses, payment plans have been worked out so that the gradual reduction and eventual elimination of the damage has already begun and progressed.

The lesson to be learned is that one must always be adequately insured to be protected against the financial calamities which can befall us in times of natural disasters.

Adequate insurance protection must be purchased to take care of medical bills, to provide replacement value in the event of car theft, auto accidents and personal injuries and homeowners coverage against burglaries and loss of valuables. Moderately affluent families with sizeable estates may find that their entire Social Security check is spent on insurance premiums. We must be continually protected, especially in later life, against eventualities, because being unprepared for disaster can ruin retirement plans.

In cases of small estates, where money is tight and heirs are on rigid budgets, it behooves the retiree to have, at least, sufficient life insurance for a decent burial. The role of life insurance in retirement planning is debatable in moderate-sized estates, but has proven effective in mitigating the expense of estate taxes in large estates.

TAXES

Retirees are still tax-paying citizens. They pay capital gains tax and regular income tax on required minimum distributions from IRAs. They pay real estate taxes as well as city and state sales taxes. Since many senior citizens have had long periods to save and invest, a sizeable portion of the nation's wealth resides in the hands of older, often retired, people.

It should be expected that in a capitalistic society some driven, productive people will earn more than the average nine-to-five types. However, it seems illogical that in the richest country in the world some families have seven homes while other working families can't afford to have one. When I hear that the wealthiest billionaires have so much money that they don't know what to do with it and so have decided to just give it away, while other folks, some veterans of our armed services, are scraping for food and shelter, it just seems wrong.

CHARITY

Charitable giving is part of world culture and especially American culture, derived from the Judeo-Christian heritage of our founding fathers. The American people are among the most generous in the world. They respond to people around the globe in times of need. Charitable giving should be part of any retirement plan that can afford such generosity. An old adage states that "charity begins at home" and loved ones should be given financial aid before anyone else. Paying a child's college tuition or helping to put a grandchild through school should be an obligation of love. To help a relative get over a rough patch, when other help is not readily available, also earns a blessing.

WILLS

When you have prepared your nest egg for a long time and have more assets than ever before, you want to make sure it passes on to where you want it to go. You then typically have to hire legal professionals to set up your estate plan and draw up a proper will. Be generous to those who have been good to you and forgiving to those who didn't know how to be. Try to be remembered kindly, with respect and dignity. In the end, family counts more than anything else. Part of your legacy will always be what your descendants will say about you. Make your lasting statement, your will, something of which you can be proud. Always include a declaration of how intense you want your final medical treatments to be (an "advance directive" or "living will"), to preserve or end your life.

PENSION PLANS

The potential retiree should be aware of the pension options available. All United States retirement plan funds are tax deferred until distributions are made, at which time the monetary distributions are taxed along with other income. Here is a brief survey of the plans available.

Basically there are two types of pension plans: *defined contribution* and *defined benefit*.

Defined contribution plans require some specific amount of money to be paid to the plan at specified intervals, while defined benefit plans invest to reach certain determined monetary goals.

Most employers prefer to offer the defined contribution plan because it is under regulatory control, with known, specific amounts which can be used to forecast budgetary needs. The defined benefit format is more apt to require adjustments, with market fluctuations, to guarantee the end result monetary amount. In times of market turbulence, unplanned-for reversals can lead to disruption of a company's balance sheet and therefore this format is shunned by many chief financial officers who do not wish to be obligated to meet defined pension payouts at possibly inconvenient times.

Most employee participation retirement accounts, known as 401(k)s, where funds are drawn from paychecks directly into tax-deferred investment accounts specifically earmarked for retirement, are of the defined contribution variety.

There are certain *balanced* plans which do offer elements of both types.

When the plan amounts have met the requirements and are retired, if distribution is not yet desired, they can be rolled over into *Individual Retirement Accounts (IRAs)* from which minimum distributions are mandatory at age seventy. These funds can be augmented with individually purchased IRAs, up to limited amounts, from banks and brokerage houses.

Corporations can also offer retirement plans based on profit sharing and stock ownership. The above-mentioned plans are some of the most popular qualified plans. For information on other qualified and unqualified plans created for specific purposes, visit www.opm.gov/retirement-services/.

WORLDWIDE EXPOSURE

Since the formation of our stock exchanges in the latter part of the eighteenth century, cumulative market value has appreciated. There have been slumps along the way, companies have failed,

industries have come and gone, but the total market has continued to grow.

There are many reasons why US markets have prospered:
population growth with greater demand for goods and services,
a major increase in American productivity fueled by the innova
tions and demands during two world wars, the relative excellence
of American ingenuity and workmanship and the American dollar replacing the pound sterling of Great Britain as the standard
currency of the world are among the most important.

More than ever in history we are now seeing emerging economies growing at a rate to become sizeable consumer states. We
now live in a global economy, where the financial well-being of
one country can readily affect the status of another, or even many.
Countries which have recognized the value of keeping their close
trading partners in good financial health have banded together
to form unions of nations. So we see European countries, historically divided and at war with each other, uniting in partnership.
The United States has made free trade agreements with Canada
and Mexico, facilitating more North American trade. The benefit to more prosperous nations in providing aid to poorer ones is
to increase their standard of living, so that this will create more
consumers for the goods and services produced by the more
developed states.

Studies have shown that younger people tend to be more
aggressive in purchasing retail items. Many large and developed countries have experienced a decrease in birth rate, while
in underdeveloped nations the birth rate has remained robust.
Fortunate countries, like the United States, a country of descendants of immigrants, have more than made up for the shortfall in
the number of new births with population increase through the
continued flow of people flocking to our shores to experience our
freedoms and prosperity. However, all developed nations recog-
nize the need to develop the natural resources of emerging states

to allow them to produce additional consumers of the goods and services offered by First World nations.

Investors should be aware of the risks and benefits when investing in foreign markets. Most investors should be cautioned that this is not an area for novices and they should be guided by financial advisers. Perhaps the greatest caution exercised would be to avoid these markets altogether, or at least to approach them through mutual funds or exchange traded funds which invest in a variety of individual stocks. Retirees and those planning for retirement should never risk more than a small portion of their retirement funds in foreign stocks. Always remember, when you buy a stock you are buying a small portion of a company. Many foreign countries have a history of governmental instability with widely fluctuating stock markets and the regulation of company earnings reporting is not as strict as in the United States. It is wise to stay away from countries which have experienced military coups and internal strife affecting corporate earnings and the very future of some enterprises.

If one is aware and determined enough to want to venture into foreign markets, perhaps the most prudent course is to buy shares of large multinational companies, which have exposure to many nations and can easily withstand a setback in one or even a few.

EDUCATION

We must also be aware that peace and educational sophistication are requirements to promote and preserve economic prosperity. There are two adversarial philosophies at work in the world: one based on great individual freedom of choice, which can more readily allow, in the negative, more violent crime and pornography, and the other of autocratic rule, which can curtail individual freedom and productivity. Under the autocratic heading we must include theocratic dictatorships, which teach imposed virtue over freedom, the nature of that virtue to be determined by those who have the power to do so. The commercial failure of the theocratic model has been well established, with the brain drain from those nations to lands of greater freedom resulting in a dearth of innovative genius remaining in lands of great natural resources. Countries dominated by autocratic rule have had to borrow technology from the lands that have allowed a more comfortable life for their masses in free societies.

TERRORISM

There is no doubt that the prime targets of terrorist groups from around the world are the centers of commerce. The best way to bring a country down is to cripple its financial structure. Take away its economic strength and you bring down its military might with it. The United States is the strongest country in the world because it is the richest. That is why our centers of finance have to be the ones that are most protected. Another September 11, 2001, would be catastrophic, not only because of the initial damage to the markets (from this we have proven to the world we can resiliently recover) but to a loss of confidence in the safety of our exchanges. Wall Street has become the symbol of market stability and safety to the world. The economic well-being of many nations rests on the safety and security of the financial systems of the United States.

Another terrorist attack involving a major American exchange would have a significant impact on retirement accounts and would be very hurtful to those retirees who do not have sufficient time to ride out the downturn.

The threat of terrorist attacks has an immediate effect on the profitability of many nations. Some of the poorest nations in the world, because of their comfortable climates, depend greatly on tourism. The threat of violence against tourists by drug lords or other uncontrolled criminal elements can greatly diminish the economy of needy nations. Not only do people shy away from visiting these otherwise desirable geographical locations, but foreign investment in the tourism and construction industries in these nations suffers. Factors such as the increased effect of crime, corruption and terrorism should be taken into account when considering investing in a foreign country.

CHAPTER 4

Investment Alternatives

For those starting out in investing for retirement, it is prudent to find out, as early as possible, what kind of investor you are. Are you better off allowing someone else to make the decisions for you or are you a take-charge person who wants to be in control? In investing, as with many other things in life, you learn from your mistakes. Sooner or later you will learn that this kind of education can be very expensive. Even if you prefer to be in command of your own finances, sometimes (especially in the beginning) it may be advisable to be guided by a professional who has the experience to steer you clear of the mistakes he or she undoubtedly has already made. Even the best investors the world has ever known have made investment mistakes. The importance lies in how you are able to respond to the disappointment of these mistakes.

There are two basic emotions involved in financial investing. During good times, when the market is going up and there is euphoria in the air, greed comes into play. In the investment world greed is good, if it is controlled. It is only dangerous when exuberance overcomes caution. One must always be aware that markets that are headed in either direction, up or down, eventually correct in the other direction. At the extreme in a down market, when stock prices tend to plummet, panic selling may occur with precipitous drops in stock prices when fear takes over.

The test of a savvy investor is how well he controls his greed and his fear. Not to lose his head, so to speak, while those around him are losing theirs. Sage advice is to be fearful when others are being reckless and to be aggressive when others are fearful: Buy when stock prices are low and sell when they are high.

The next factor may be as much based on strategy as it is on emotions and that is risk aversion. It is more prudent to panic early and take a small loss, which can be easily recouped later, rather than panicking late in the downturn and having to struggle to overcome a substantial loss. Sell today and have enough to buy back a significant amount of shares at a lower price tomorrow. Always remember that when a stock depreciates in value and you can buy it back at a cheaper price, if your loss is measured you may be able to recapture the same number or even more of the same shares than you had originally.

If the investor is in control of his investment portfolio, he must always be aware of his limits, when a loss is no longer tolerable. You marry a man or a woman till death do you part, but not a stock or fund of stocks. Falling in love with shares to the detriment of common-sense investing is gambling on recovery, not prudent investing. It is better to cut your losses and get out early. America has suffered through two severe depressions in eighty years, where portfolios have been wiped out because people held onto investments too long.

Investors can make money in down markets by selling short. When you sell short you actually never truly own the stock shares, you merely borrow them with the hope of buying them back at a cheaper price later. You are betting that the stock price will go down. If the price continues to appreciate, your losses can be large. This has been made much easier in today's markets than it was in years gone by, with newer investment vehicles available through brokerage house innovation. Since the markets have a greater tendency to go up, selling short should be understood to be a temporary investment only, best made by sophisticated investors who have the time to follow the market closely and can deftly get out when things turn around.

INVESTMENT VEHICLES

Investing in individual stocks requires research, which some like to do, but many others would not like to spend their leisure hours this way. Things unknown to the unsuspecting investor can reduce the stock price of a given company. Sudden tax or other penalties, previously undisclosed expenses, lawsuit settlements and a myriad of other factors can alter earning projections and may be reported too late for the individual investor to keep from suffering a sizeable loss.

Recognizing this difficulty for the small investor who would otherwise depend on the expertise of his broker, many years ago when fees were high the brokerage houses developed mutual funds. These funds invested in many stocks, allowing the small investor exposure to a segment, or all, of the market at more reasonable rates. Since there are fees and expenses to pay for the expertise of those running the funds, approximately 80 percent of mutual funds lag behind the general market in performance. Only 20 percent, with the best fund managers, are successful in beating the total market each year. It varies year to year which funds beat the average. Only the most adept managers come in ahead of the market year after year. Recognizing this difficulty, the fund companies developed index funds, which track the market and, since they are passively managed, they require less fees and expenses to be taken out for management.

Attempting to reduce fees further, in order to attract more advanced investors shopping for investment vehicles which cost less, companies developed exchange traded funds (ETFs). These are baskets of stocks representing given industries or the total market, which are just periodically allocated, but usually not actively managed and therefore carry lower fees than mutual funds.

They also differ from mutual funds in that they are traded on the major stock exchanges just like individual stocks. Investment firms usually regard mutual funds to be relatively long-term investments and frown on their being traded frequently, because this causes them to sell stocks at inconvenient times. Another advantage of ETFs is that they can be bought or sold at any time of the day, while mutual fund transactions are executed only after the trading day has been completed. This can be disadvantageous in major market swings.

There are many other trading vehicles available, which should be reserved only for the retirement plans of the most knowledgeable investors with the time and inclination to follow the markets on a daily basis. Options allow investors to buy the equivalent of a great number of shares with a much smaller outlay of cash, taking on the risk of the possible total loss of the amount invested.

Currency trading and the carry trade, where the bonds of countries with lower interest rates are traded for bonds from countries with higher interest rates and the difference in interest pocketed, can be most profitable for those who know how to handle such vehicles. However, this requires expertise.

Investments in art, precious gems and metals have made fortunes for some people who were astute enough to wait for periods of sizeable appreciation to sell. The average person with a modest portfolio should consider ownership in this area with only a small fraction of the funds intended for retirement. In retirement accounts where cash flow is required to pay for living expenses, a sizeable or usually even a major portion of the investments should be in income-producing instruments. Hard objects and equities with no, or meager, yields should be relegated to a minor role in such plans or none at all.

Many ultraconservative investors, knowing their adversity to risk taking, especially if they produce sufficient income with enough needed growth, hold no common stocks in their portfolios. This is fine for those who have wealth beyond projected needs, but most individuals need retirement plans with a balanced approach in stocks and/or stock funds, as well as fixed-income vehicles to meet the requirements of an unknowable length of retirement.

Among fixed-income investments are savings accounts, certificates of deposit (CDs), money market accounts and United States treasury securities, available through banks and investment firms. These carry the guarantee of principal backed by the United States government. Unless held in a tax sheltered account, interest earned by these savings vehicles is usually subject to taxation.

Non-guaranteed income-producing investments include corporate bonds, income-producing common stocks, such as utilities and preferred stocks, some of which may include a provision to be converted to common stock in the future. Since this group of investments carries a greater risk of loss of value than the secured investments listed above, the interest and dividend yield is usually higher, sometimes substantially so. Bonds are rated as to level of safety: A, B or C. Many financial advisers recommend only bonds rated in the single A or above category—the highest being AAA—for retirement accounts, while others do consider BBB level bonds to be of investment grade. The lower the grade, the higher the projected yield. In investing, the greater the risk the greater the promise of reward.

Bonds issued by states, cities or their agencies, known as tax-free municipal bonds, are not subject to federal taxation and to the residents of those states income earned is not subject to state taxes as well. These bonds should never be held in retirement plans which are already tax deferred, since the tax advantages are thus lost. Occasionally, taxable municipal bonds are issued, which usually have higher yields than the tax-free variety and in my experience are highly prized by bond buyers for retirement accounts. Although tax-free municipal bonds are not appropriate to be purchased for IRAs and other retirement modalities, they are an excellent investment bought with other available funds, to augment eventual income free of taxation.

I now will give some advice which is contrary to that which you may get from an investment firm selling mutual funds. I do not recommend bond mutual funds. Whereas individual bonds have an expiration date, which assures you that you will get back the amount of money you expected to when you bought the bond at the time you sell it, the price of a bond fund fluctuates with the rise and fall of interest rates. If you are reasonably sure that you can exist on the interest rate of an individual bond and will not need to sell it before it expires, then, unless the bond defaults, you have a relatively safe investment and your investment amount will be returned to you. However, with a bond fund with no expiration date, the price you receive on the date you may have to sell it may be below what you paid when you bought it. If the interest rates rise substantially you may take a loss, even beyond the total of the interest payments you have received, depending on the price change and how long you kept the bond fund.

The contrary argument you will receive from the bond fund sellers is that buying a large number of bonds in a fund is a safer investment because companies like General Motors and even cities, like Detroit, have declared bankruptcy with a significant loss to bond holders. The fixed-income investor has to weigh the pros and cons of which investment vehicle to choose. This is why only highly rated bonds are advisable for retirement accounts.

INVESTMENT PLANNING

Cognizant men and women all over the world are taking precautions to extend their lives. Many watch what they eat and how much they weigh. They exercise daily and get on the scales routinely. Recent insurance industry actuarial studies project that the average couple, when they both reach sixty years of age, will have at least one member live to be over ninety years old.[5] Many in their seventies today may live well into their nineties or beyond. With better dietary habits and advanced medical care, life expectancy is continually increasing. Some people who plan to retire soon may spend up to one-third to one-quarter of the total of their entire lives in retirement. This has greatly alarmed government planners in America, because only 50 percent of people are participating in retirement plans. Even many who are enrolled in qualified plans will have insufficient funds available to sustain a lengthy retirement. With the population growing older and more people approaching retirement age, if they have not planned for an adequate retirement, this can become a national nightmare with an ever-increasing number of senior citizens living below the poverty line.

When secure pension benefits, such as those that most American government workers and some other countries enjoy, and Social Security payments together are adequate to sustain an acceptable lifestyle, there is no problem. However, when outside income is projected to be insufficient to maintain a desired standard of living, it is the individual's responsibility to have the foresight to formulate a plan early enough in life to amass the wealth necessary for a successful retirement.

The earlier the plan is put in place, the more aggressive the early investor should be. The more time available before the funds are drawn upon, the greater the resilience in overcoming mistakes and setbacks. When small amounts are present, then the losses are also small and insignificant in the long run. However, when money piles up and grows substantial, as the investor ages the investments should grow more conservative, because large losses close to retirement time can derail retirement plans. Early on, greater allocation should be in common stocks and stock funds; later on the majority should be in fixed-income vehicles. Ideally, after retiring, a family should be able to expect adequate income for their living expenses from income-producing investments, while depending on equities to provide sufficient appreciation to at least keep up with inflation. This will guarantee that the retirees will enjoy an acceptable standard of living for the rest of their lives.

INVESTMENT PHILOSOPHIES

With the understanding that over the years even large and well-established companies have failed and fortunes have been won and lost by seasoned investors, you have to come to understand where your own best interests lie. How much risk can you tolerate? How much time and effort are you willing or able to devote to managing your finances? Do you want to micromanage your retirement accounts or simply turn the whole thing over to someone else? In that case, can you tolerate someone else mismanaging your accounts? A secure retirement may very well depend on you getting to know yourself enough to make the right decisions.

There are basically two retirement philosophies: passive and active. If you feel you are not willing or able to make the needed, sometimes day-by-day, investment decisions required for positive results, then you should choose a passive role. Either employ an investment advisory service and allow them to invest for you directly or guide you to do what they advise, or buy into several mutual funds which address different sectors, making periodic monetary contributions to ride out the ups and downs of the market. Many mutual funds are chartered only to buy stocks and are not allowed to short sell, as is beneficial in a down market; therefore, the only way to prosper with these investment vehicles is to buy while the market is going down as well as when it is going up, thus averaging out share costs. As historically the market has gone up over time, this course should be profitable. The profits may not be as sizeable as in the case of an actively managed portfolio where timely decisions are made when to buy and when to sell. If those decisions are not well timed, the outcome could be no better or even worse.

Actively managing a sizeable portfolio which has appreciated over the years can be a time-consuming endeavor. If done aggressively, trading in and out of positions with market swings, it can become a job in itself. If you are inclined after retirement to take on this kind of activity and can handle the stress of sometimes failing, with the subsequent second-guessing that is part of the game, you may be rewarded with the periodic joy of victory. If you are a competitive person with the desire for challenge who can treat this like a game, you will be haunted by the losses and exhilarated by the gains. The object is, as with any sport, to win a lot more than you lose. No one, not even the very best, is right every time.

Making money in an up market, where the Dow Jones daily listings of the share price of thirty of the world's largest industrial companies are routinely going up, is relatively easy, because a rising market lifts the price of most good stocks, like a rising tide lifts all boats. The object of successful investing is not only to take advantage of an up market, but also to limit losses in a down market. Ultimately success or failure may rest not on how much you make in good times, but on how little you lose in bad times. Like in many sports, the offense scores the points, but the defense wins the game. Careful maneuvering to avoid serious setbacks may require active management.

Therefore, the final decision as to how to manage your finances depends on how much time, effort and emotion you are willing to invest. As with most things, you will get out of it, in measure, what you are willing to put in. If you are very involved elsewhere or for health or other reasons cannot devote what is needed, then the wise decision is to be a passive investor.

INVESTMENT STRATEGY

The greatest financial fear of retirement is outliving your money. Having to live poor after experiencing much better times earlier is a horrid future to anticipate. Having to scrimp on necessities, especially after enjoying relative luxuries earlier, should be considered unacceptable. Therefore every effort should be made to eliminate such an eventuality, even if it means cutting back on desired extravagances earlier in life. No one knows how long they will live. As people live longer than ever now, if you are enjoying reasonably good health, plan to outlive your oldest dead relative. If you don't live that long, then leave what is left to your heirs, but at all costs do not be foolish enough to squander your wealth. Living out your last years near or below the poverty line should be an unimaginable fate for any family. Many people, some famous celebrities, have made questionable investment decisions and impoverished themselves, having to go begging for aid from friends and family. The primary goal of any sound investment strategy is not to run out of adequate income no matter how long you may live.

The more money you accumulate, the more apt you are to attract those who would offer you "get richer" schemes and business propositions. Do not fall prey to anything that comes from unestablished sources. Deal only with accredited brokerage firms and government-insured banks. Be suspicious of so-called "business managers" who seek you out. Always research the background of any potential partnerships. In my experience, if you join as a limited partner, it is the general partners who take a major share of the profits. Avoid speculative ventures. Recall that if a deal seems to be too good to be true, it usually is. True windfalls are rare. You may be fortunate enough to find a good broker who offers sound advice, but on many occasions you will discover that these people are just salesmen who are trying to sell you whatever their broker-age firm wants to get rid of and to gain large fees for themselves.

There are very good reasons for investing by yourself. The most important are safety and low transaction fees. If you invest online with a well-established brokerage firm which handles bil-lions of dollars of customer assets and has the most sophisticated anti-hacking equipment available, there is typically much less chance of being swindled than if you place your hard-earned cash in the hands of an investment manager. During the past few years, many hedge funds run by supposed market gurus have severely underperformed the general market; a number have gone com-pletely out of business, resulting in crushing losses for their cus-tomers. We were all horrified to learn of the massive Ponzi schemes perpetrated on wealthy, well-educated and sophisticated socialites and celebrities by trusted advisers they had dealt with honestly for many years. Schemes which were supposed to be regulated by the Securities and Exchange Commission (SEC) were allowed to exist making no investments at all, just taking money from later inves-tors to pay the alleged profits owed to earlier ones. Even charitable institutions, supposedly supervised by boards of directors, were robbed of many millions of dollars. These victims will have to set-tle for pennies on the dollar in the final accounting. If prominent individuals and institutions, who have the financial means to hire agents to advise them, were so taken in by charlatans, shouldn't the average investor be very concerned about who is caring for his or her retirement money?

After each bad investment I make, after chastising myself, I console myself by realizing how much more furious I'd be if someone else had lost this money for me. I jokingly tell my wife that I will never again let anyone else lose any of our money; I do a good enough job of that myself.

If you watch your investments closely and buy and sell shares actively, making many trades annually, the brokerage fees can become exorbitant if you use a full-service broker. Whatever advantage is gained by the recommendations you act upon may be done away with by the costs. Trading online, your transaction fees are a tiny fraction of what a full-service broker charges and after a period of time the savings can become quite substantial.

Online investing is also more convenient for busy people. Many stories have been told about the inaccessibility of brokers at vital times. Being able to respond promptly to market moves may be the difference between a profit and a loss. In this age of technological innovation it is unthinkable to have to wait for a broker to call you back to make a transaction. People on the go, either at work or elsewhere, can trade from a smartphone or a tablet if they are away from their computers and the trades are executed virtually instantaneously.

DIVERSIFICATION

We have all heard the old saying, "Don't put all your eggs in one basket." It has been reported that America's foremost investor and one of the world's richest men, Warren Buffet, modified that somewhat when he was quoted as saying, "It's alright to put all your eggs in one basket, if you watch the basket closely." Most of us are not professional investors and just don't have the time or inclination to watch our baskets that carefully and therefore have to diversify our investment portfolios.

Most people feel that by investing in mutual funds they already have diversification, and many do. However it is prudent to know what stocks are in your mutual funds. Many funds invest in the same stocks. So even if you own several funds, hoping to be invested in different sectors of the market, you may in fact just be buying and owning the same stocks. Therefore, if you are a mutual fund investor you should adjust your holdings so that you have representation in many sectors of the economy.

Conversely, some financial analysts feel that many mutual funds, each containing positions in hundreds of stocks, lag in performance behind the market in general because they are over-diversified. In times of down markets there just aren't that many company stocks appreciating in value to justify holding so many losing positions. If you become aware that you own mutual funds that are underperforming their peer averages, you might be better off switching to index funds, which invest in the most prominent companies of their respective markets.

There are thousands of mutual funds and exchange traded funds to choose from and it can become confusing which to select. If your plan allows you the freedom to choose, but your schedule doesn't afford you the time to spend on the research required, it is probably wise to choose to invest in index funds. Exchange traded index funds are available that track the Standard & Poor's, Nasdaq and Dow Jones Indexes. The Standard & Poor's indexes contain large corporations, both national and international. The Nasdaq indexes are mainly made up of companies involved with technology and the Dow Jones Average index contains thirty of the most prominent industrial companies.

Besides exchange traded index funds, which increase or decrease in value along with the markets, there are also exchange traded index funds which increase or decrease two or three times what the markets do. So more aggressive traders can realize two or three times greater profits or losses. These modalities should be used with caution and only by those investors with the ability to buy and sell rapidly. An old adage attributed to one of the Rothschild barons seems appropriate in regard to these multiplied index funds, "Treat the stock market like a hot bath: get in quickly and get out quickly."

Those investors who feel confident enough to trade in individual stocks should heed the recommendation of many honest advisers and never put more than five percent of total assets in any one company stock. Responsible ownership of an individual stock requires watching for any news which may alter the bottom line of that company and following the share price closely.

AGGRESSIVE MANEUVERS

The degree of aggressive allocation of funds should be related to the time remaining for appreciation. Younger workers can choose, if they have the option, to be fully or near fully funded in equities, while older investors should usually be more cautious and accumulate more interest and dividend-producing vehicles for income. However, when planning for retirement has started in the middle years or later, a different approach may be advisable.

It is a sobering fact that nearly half of American retirees will run out of money while still alive. In recognition of this, those starting late in life have to put away the maximum allowed by law for those fifty years of age and older. This may also cause a welcome decrease in the tax bill if the employee is eligible for a tax-deferred plan. It will also require previously avoided financial sacrifice. Since equities, or equity funds, historically yield greater returns than fixed-income vehicles like treasuries and CDs, people who start to save and invest late in life almost have to be more fully invested in more risky investments to reach the monetary requirements for an adequate retirement.

This sounds almost paradoxical, advising those most vulnerable to gamble the most. However, we must treat the lost time of investing like a financial loss. When you lose 50 percent of an investment you have to make 100 percent back to break even. Playing catchup is a risky business but the alternative is inadequate funds being available when needed.

Hopefully, when you reach an age perhaps beyond what you dreamed you would ever get to and you foresee a bleak, impoverished future, you will summon the wisdom to plan better, save more and live more wisely. This should include watching your investments closely and avoiding pitfalls so that your nest egg grows, because additional losses could prove fatal to your retirement plans. To avoid this difficulty, begin to plan for retirement as early as possible.

SPECIFIC INVESTMENTS

Almost all major investment firms offer a wide variety of mutual funds for the passive investor which can be followed in the financial sections of the daily newspapers or online. More aggressive investors, who feel that they are capable stock pickers or believe that they have a reliable, astute professional to guide them, should pay rigorous attention to the markets and devote significant time to research.

For those retirees who have IRAs which allow tax-deferred investing and/or those who have other self-directed retirement plans, another avenue of investing is available. If you wish to have firm control of your financial accounts but do not have the expertise available to you to continually know which individual stocks to buy or sell, then you should consider being invested in significant segments of the market instead of individual stocks. While more passive investors can do this with index mutual funds, more active investors may desire the greater flexibility and lower costs of exchange traded funds, which trade on the exchanges the same way individual stocks do.

Over the years many large and famous companies have gone out of business, while the market, as a whole, has continued to flourish. So there really is safety in numbers. If you are not willing or able to put in the time to study charts and truly become proficient at learning the details of the workings of individual companies, I suggest you invest in groups of stocks. You must always remember that when you buy a stock you are buying a small part of a company. When you go into business you should have all the facts and figures concerning that business and not just place your money at risk on someone's advice. The advice might be self-serving and not for your best benefit. For the cautious investor who wants to guard against mistakes, unless you have detailed, positive information about a company or the information comes from a tried and true source, don't invest in individual companies unless you have developed the expertise to routinely pick winners.

Stocks are listed and traded by their symbols: Ford Motor Company is F, General Motors is GM, the Walt Disney Company is DIS and so on. Most companies listed on the New York Stock Exchange, like the three mentioned, have one to three letters in their symbols. Many stocks listed on the Nasdaq Exchange have four (or five) letters in their symbols; Apple Inc. is listed on the Nasdaq as AAPL. Exchange traded funds also have symbols.

Among the most frequently traded index ETFs, the one containing the thirty stocks comprising the Dow Jones Industrial Average is recognized by the symbol DIA; the one involved with the five hundred stocks of the Standard & Poor's Index has the symbol SPY and for one hundred Nasdaq listed stocks it's QQQ. Most of the companies contained in the three funds mentioned above are considered to be large companies; a fund for smaller companies has the symbol IWM.

Exchange traded funds are known as ETFs; the Dow Jones Industrial Average is just called the Dow and the Standard and Poor's 500 is abbreviated as the S&P 500.

The more aggressive investor, including numerous professionals who are required to try to produce better results than the general market, invest in ETFs that advance twice as much as the markets. The ETF that doubles the results of the Dow has the symbol DDM; the one that doubles the S&P 500 is listed as SSO; the two times the Nasdaq is QLD and for smaller stocks it's MVV.

For even more aggressive trading there are ETFs that return triple the results of the indexes: SPXL for large companies and TNA for smaller ones.

ETF trading has become a very popular way to invest in large segments of the market without the expenses and restrictions of mutual funds and not requiring the time and expertise needed to pick individual stock winners.

When you buy a bond issued by a company, unlike a stock, you do not own a piece of that company; you are merely loaning the company money to help finance some aspect of its business. Except when held in tax-deferred accounts, the interest received from corporate bonds is subject to annual taxation. Remember that municipal bonds are usually free of federal taxes and, if purchased by residents of the same state, are usually not subject to state taxes. On occasion, municipalities can issue taxable bonds as well. Since taxable bonds carry an additional financial burden, they have to compete for potential bond buyers by offering higher interest rates than tax-free bonds. Bonds are rated as to safety by rating agencies. Safety is determined by the relative financial strength of the bond issuer. Other factors involved in the assessment of security are whether the bond is insured, backed up by a sinking fund or if the issuer has the ability to tax or collect tolls to secure the money necessary to make timely interest payments and return the full amount on the expiration or due date.

Bonds are loans for a specified time period. They promise to pay a specified interest on specific dates, usually at quarterly or semi-annual intervals, and they promise to return a defined amount on the expiration date. If they fail to do that, they are said to be in default. Some bonds carry call dates. If the bond issuer, for whatever reason, feels it is financially advantageous, on a prearranged date the bond may be called (prematurely expired) and the promised call date amount returned to the lender. The call date amount may or may not be the same as the due day amount. All these specifications are spelled out in the prospectus (a brochure of details) for the buyer to be aware of prior to purchase. Some bonds offer protection against being called.

Bond ratings determine the amount of interest a bond will pay. The safer the bond, the less interest to be expected. The greater the risk, the greater the return, so that a AAA rated municipal bond usually would have a much lower yield than an A rated corporate bond. Bonds rated C or lower are known as junk bonds and return the highest interest rates. Not all junk bonds carry the implied risk. Some very young companies with promising futures, which haven't established a good credit rating as yet, are forced to borrow money at high rates and their bonds just don't merit anything higher than a C rating. Since the value of a bond, the amount you would have to pay if you wanted to buy it, fluctuates with the interest rate it offers, as the rating of the young company goes up and its bonds pay less interest, the value of its bonds go up. If you buy a bond when it is C rated and sell it after it goes up and becomes B rated or higher you will realize a profit. Since you would not only have received a high interest rate for the period you owned the bond, but also a capital appreciation upon the sale, buying a junk bond could be a good investment. However, it takes time and effort to gain the expertise to determine which low-rated bonds to buy and which to stay away from.

For those who want the relative safety of bonds, which do not usually fluctuate in price as much as stocks and cannot, or will not, devote that which is needed to buy individual bonds, the alternate choice is to invest in bond mutual funds. The diversification of a bond fund protects against the major loss which may be incurred with a single bond default, the safety of many investments versus the one. However, the price value of bonds fluctuates with interest rates and the value of a bond fund adjusts accordingly, so as interest rates go up, the value of the fund goes down. Whereas individual bonds have expiration dates when repayment in full is due, bond funds have no due dates and when the fund is sold, it may be at a loss. With individual bonds you have a reasonable expectation that you will get back, besides the interest promised, the full amount you invested. With bond funds you have less of such assurance. An advantage of bond funds is that if you don't need the money, instead of receiving periodic interest payments, you can choose to have the money buy additional shares of the fund. This can develop into an automatic reinvestment plan over time.

The profit created by a newly-issued bond held over the lifetime of the bond is solely in the interest produced. Therefore, one should always be aware of what can subtract from that profit. Newly issued bonds are sold at par ($100.00) in $1000 increments and any transaction costs are already calculated into the sales price. You get $100.00 rated value for $100.00 invested. When you buy a bond from a broker's portfolio, which has been issued earlier, this is referred to as a secondary market purchase and the broker is entitled to an additional transaction fee, reducing your actual yield. If during the time between the issuance of the bond and the purchase the interest rates change, you may pay more or less than $100. If you see a bond price listed at $101.76, it means that interest rates have gone down since the initial sale and you will have to pay 1.76 percent more than the original buyer did for the same number of bonds. If you want to buy a bond listed on the secondary market at $99.37, the price having come down because interest rates have gone up, you can purchase the bond at a discount.

Both safety rating change and interest rate fluctuation influence the sale price of bonds and both should be taken into account when considering buying any one bond. The effect of transaction fees on yield expectations should also be considered. During a period of rising interest rates, as the value of bonds fall, the degree of need for the income from bond interest should determine how many, if any, of the bonds should be sold to realize a current profit, which will vanish as prices continue to go down.

Preferred stocks differ from common stocks by having different ownership rights in the company and act like bonds in delivering dividend income, usually higher than that offered by the common stock. Many common stocks of aggressively growing companies offer little or no dividends. Preferred stocks react to marketplace and interest rate fluctuations. Convertible preferred stocks can be converted into common stocks when certain criteria are met.

A technique to overcome the fluctuation of interest rate effects on bond prices, to promote stability of price value and desired interest return, is called *layering*. Usually bonds with longer maturities have greater yields than bonds of similar rating which come due much sooner. In order to stabilize returns and ride out market swings, continuing periodic purchases of bonds of varying maturities can mitigate these undulations. The creation of so-called bond layers in time will grow and mature into a collection of many varied bonds, which average out over up and down markets to a portfolio with a stable value and yielding an adequate anticipated income.

When you buy a bond at a discount to par value and it is called at par or better, or comes due at par or better, you will realize a taxable gain, even if it's a bond where the interest paid is tax free. For example, if you buy ten bonds at $98.50 and pay $9850 plus a $50 brokerage fee, for a total of $9900 and then sell at $100.00 (par) for $10,000, you will have a $100 taxable gain. Similarly, if you buy 10 bonds at $108.50 and pay $10,850 plus a $50 transaction fee, for a total of $10,900, and then the bonds are called or come due at par, so that you receive only $10,000, you have sustained a $900 loss.

The interest earned annually from a mixture of bonds, held individually or in funds, can be counted on to contribute, along with common and preferred stock dividends, to the income a family requires after retirement as a supplement to Social Security and other pension benefits. Common stock appreciation should be counted on to grow with and even exceed inflation, to assure that the retired family will not have to sell assets prematurely and frighteningly outlive their money.

The challenge is to learn and apply formulas which have been devised by experienced financial analysts over the course of the years to know how much is needed in different situations and how it is to be allocated.

ASSET ALLOCATION

The proper balancing of different types of investments, so that after retirement there is a steady, adequate stream of income as well as a sufficient amount of growth potential to be able to handle emergencies and cost of living increases, is one of the prime concerns of retirement planning.

At different times of life the situation of the future retiree will change and the retirement portfolio should be adjusted to accommodate these changes. Earlier in life, when the investment horizon is long term, more aggressive investments like higher-risk stocks and high-interest-paying lower-rated bonds could be included in the investment strategy after a base of savings has been established. Later on, a more conservative approach is usually recommended. As the nest egg grows and more substantial sums are at risk, more dividend-paying so-called "blue chip" stocks and high-rated bonds should be added. When the time for retirement grows near, most of the assets should be invested in income-producing vehicles to generate the money needed for living expenses, while a lesser segment of the investments should be allocated in growth vehicles, like stocks.

The first move in any retirement plan should always be the limiting, or even better still, the total elimination of debt.

The second step should be the accumulation of sufficient funds in government-secured savings or money market accounts to be able to survive six months of no, or insufficient, income. While worker's compensation and other disability insurance benefits may help with the bare necessities, at a time of health problems they may not be adequate for all needs. Even if the benefit checks pay the rent or the mortgage and buy food, which they may not always do, they most likely will not pay for needed home repairs or other expenses.

The plan must always prepare for emergencies: illnesses, job loss, natural disasters, inadequate insurance coverage, legal fees and a myriad of other potential devastations can befall a family in a lifetime. The "It won't happen to me" attitude can be ruinous. Adequate preparation can mitigate loss of income and loss of property, just not loss of life. Even in that terrible eventuality, with adequate foresight the family could handle a respectful funeral without undue sacrifice.

The ideal retirement planning should be started as soon as the individual is through with schooling and becomes employed. Forced sacrifice should be initiated by enrolling in an employer-sponsored 401(k) plan which takes money out of each paycheck, earmarked specifically for retirement saving. Ideally, the maximum allowed should be deducted, so that the nest egg will be given a chance to grow to the amount needed for a comfortable retirement. This takes discipline, patience and sacrifice. These savings, for people making a modest living, can mean giving up some desired things while young; however, it may also mean getting some desired things when older. Placing as much money as possible in growth vehicles at a young age is of the greatest importance and cannot be overemphasized.

In an environment where even long-term (twenty to thirty-year) investment grade bonds yield only 4 percent or so, $1,000,000 is required to earn $40,000 annually. The average middle-income family is almost required to become wealthy in order to continue to enjoy a decent lifestyle after retirement. While this may seem like a daunting task, it really isn't, if the plan is adopted early and adhered to stringently over its full course.

Laet's say an average American worker begins at an entry-level wage in his or her twenties and progresses, earning reasonable increases in salary, contributing the maximum allowed by law to a retirement plan, invested prudently. Considering that index funds return on average about 7 percent a year, after forty years, upon reaching retirement age, depending on income, the amount accumulated may be over $1,000,000. Ideally, in forty years or so, every worker saving for retirement will be a millionaire. Sadly, it has been estimated that today the average funded retirement plan has about one third the required amount and these people can look forward to being in dire straits unless they keep on working.

TAXATION

Middle management employees, small business owners, professionals and others who earn sufficient amounts to have savings beyond what they have accumulated in tax-deferred retirement accounts, may rightly be concerned by the taxes they have to pay. After age seventy and a half, IRA owners are required to take annually calculated minimal distributions, which are taxed as regular income. These distribution amounts increase with the age of the individual. If the retirement accounts have grown to a sizeable amount, then the distributions could grow to exceed family expenses, and have to be invested. If taxation is a concern, then investment of this money in tax-exempt municipal bonds should be a consideration to avoid adding to the tax burden. Municipal bonds usually are a safe investment—most bonds carry an investment grade rating. They are investments in local and statewide agencies, school systems, waterworks, toll roads and airports, and represent loans to facilitate these projects. Long ago it was recognized that cities and states could not pay for all the services that their citizens required through taxation alone and so, to ensure that bonds issued by municipalities would be desirable to compete against taxable bonds, they were given tax-free status.

Those individuals who wish to purchase safe investments, the income from which is totally tax free, while at the same time supporting their own or adjacent communities, should buy bonds from their home city and state. Not only is this a good investment, it is good citizenship.

CHAPTER 5

Financial Formulas for Retirement

The makeup of retirement plans differs as to type of plan, age of the individual and other factors. To create a specific model with percentages that work, I will introduce formulas for the typical self-directed IRA. Whether bought directly or rolled over from expired pension plans, IRAs contain a large portion of retirement funding.

The question usually asked about asset allocation is, how much should I have in stocks and how much in bonds? An old, tried-and-true rule of thumb teaches that you should subtract your age from one hundred; that is the percent you should have invested in corporate equities and the balance in income-producing investments. Using that formula, at age thirty you should be invested 70 percent in stocks or stock funds and 30 percent in bonds, bond funds, CDs or other income-producing investments. At fifty years of age, you should be equally invested in stocks and bonds and at retirement age you should not have more than 40 percent at risk in the stock market. When there is need for additional income after retirement, an even lower percentage should be invested in stocks. If at all possible, some amount should always be allocated for growth, but this becomes actuarially moot at an advanced age; so that folks in their nineties, unless they have sufficient assets they want to leave to their heirs, can be entirely invested in income-producing securities.

These figures are based on having begun investing at a young age. If investment is begun later in life and a catchup process has to be instituted to achieve desired results, investments have to be more aggressive. Either a greater percent has to be allocated to stocks, which have historically produced greater returns than bonds, or higher-risk stock investments, such as in those ETFs which return twice or three times the market performance, have to be made. If an aggressive investment course is chosen, the investor has to be cautious about the greater risk of substantial loss to an already under-funded account and that increased attention has to be paid.

LATE INVESTORS

Americans have enjoyed great stability, both in their government and in financial markets. Because of this optimism and a lack of fear of future events, many Americans are spenders, not savers. The appetite for more and more goods has become insatiable. On average, most people accumulate more stuff than needed. Many citizens, from different walks of life, appear not to care what tomorrow may bring and live only for the pleasures of today. This has led to an impending crisis. As the population is aging, more and more people who are approaching retirement age have insufficient money saved to finance anything near a comfortable retirement.

The Japanese, whose homeland took a terrible battering from two atomic bomb attacks during World War II and whose stock market lost 80 percent over the past decades, save much more than Americans do. Watching your stock market plunge from 39,000 to be sitting at 17,000 as of November 2014 can be quite sobering. Loss of faith in the financial systems of government causes a greater understanding of the need for self-reliance and a flight to safety.

Most young workers of today have been made aware of the need for investing for retirement. In America, for instance, some are offered 401(k) plans at work, so they automatically have investments made for them on each payday. The greater problem is with older workers who have neglected to prepare and have less time to accumulate the money required to finance their retirement needs.

Many major American investment companies have recognized the plight of these investors and have advertised widely to gain their attention. No group of future retirees need financial advisers more than the relatively unsophisticated investors who begin to invest late in life.

Those who start late and feel that they can manage their own investments must be aware that they require the utilization of more aggressive modalities which need closer scrutiny. They should choose funds with records of substantial growth over the years and for retirement income. Instead of bonds they should rely on the higher yield of utility-like stocks, which lately have returned 5 to 6 percent in dividends. If an even higher yield is needed, then one might consider a company which invests in a group of preferred stocks, which lately has yielded 6 to 7 percent. Greater income-producing funds and real estate investment trusts (REITs) carry the danger of greater price fluctuation. One must be aware that if the price decreases a greater percentage than the yield, there is an actual loss.

Safety of capital must always be a prime consideration, especially when the money is limited and one has to resort to aggressive trading.

DELAY OF BENEFITS

If there is not a dire need for the money, in the United States, Social Security payments should be taken at the most advanced age feasible, ideally at seventy, the oldest age allowed by the government. At age seventy you would collect approximately one third more than you would at sixty-five and almost twice as much as you would receive if you chose to get early payments starting at age sixty-two. In assessing the value of Social Security payments, remember they are taxed along with other income and that has to be factored into their monetary value and when you should decide to receive the monthly checks.

Social Security can be a strong adjunct to the retirement nest egg. Two married professionals, earning mid-level salaries, who have paid in the maximum required in deductions from each paycheck for the entire length of their employment, can expect at age seventy, together, to receive over $50,000 a year, minus what is deducted for Medicare.

ALLOTMENT FORMULAS

Probably the most common questions asked about retirement finances are, "How much will I need?" and "Will I run out of money before I die?"

There is a formula which can be adapted for different income levels, using different percentages in the equation. This is necessary, because a family earning $50,000 per year needs about 100 percent of its present income to maintain its usual lifestyle in retirement, while one with an aggregate income of $100,000 can make it on 80 percent, one making $300,000 on 70 percent, and one making $500,000 will do well on 60 percent. A family fortunate enough to have an annual income of $1,000,000 can get along on 50 percent or less. People who have an average wage over $1,000,000, unless they have huge dependency problems, usually do not need any formulas.

In the United States, the retirement age has remained at sixty-five years while life expectancy has constantly gone up. If a woman lives into her nineties, she will spend one third of her life in retirement. This is putting a great strain on the Social Security system. Gradually, the government will attempt to push back the age of eligibility for Social Security benefits out of absolute necessity; otherwise, the system will go broke. It's all but inevitable. We have to plan for this or we will be greatly disappointed.

A reasonable expectation is that during the next generation the considered retirement age will be seventy. This will be a hardship for laborers who would struggle greatly to physically adapt, but that is a problem for social scientists to ponder. Retraining programs to convert to less strenuous occupations will have to be implemented to allow people to earn a living until they retire. On the other hand, those people who can afford it can retire at any age, if Social Security benefits make up an insignificant portion of their retirement income.

The age at which you retire is very important in calculating how much money you will require. Other factors include credit for Social Security and other income, like rents from owned real estate, trust funds and other sources. Each $30,000 in income is given a $1,000,000 credit.

The formulated amounts are approximate figures, calculated to place the retiree in an excellent position to enjoy a comfortable retirement, come what may. The formula for how much money is required at different income levels, at differing retirement ages, is as follows:

The age at the time of retirement should be subtracted from 100 and that number then multiplied by the desired annual income and the additional income credit subtracted from that result.

Using this formula, a retiree with a calculated need of $50,000 annually, based on the 100 percent need of a previous recent average earnings of $50,000 per year, who retires at age sixty-five, would subtract 65 from 100 leaving a multiplier of 35 (100−65 = 35). Thirty-five times $50,000 would give us a figure of $1,750,000. If Social Security plus additional annual incomes come somewhere near $30,000, a $1,000,000 credit is applicable, giving us a total need of $750,000. These are ideal figures and it is easy to recognize the difficulty an average family of four living on an annual income of $50,000 would have in amassing three quarters of a million dollars. However, if that retiree worked until age seventy, accruing greater Social Security benefits, and reduced the need ratio to 95 percent, then the figures would be 100–70 = 30, 30 x $45,000 = $1,350,000 and $1,350,000–$1,000,000 = $350,000. $350,000 is still a daunting figure at this income level, but more manageable if an investment plan is begun early and adhered to.

Now let us address those retirees with an annual income of $100,000, with an estimated need ratio of 80 percent, requiring an annual retirement income of $80,000 per year. They retire at sixty-five and leave a balance of $1,300,000 ($2,800,000–1,500,000). With a fully-funded investment plan, a family with an annual income of $100,000 can achieve a retirement nest egg of $1,300,000 with some sacrifice. However, if retirement is delayed until age seventy, then the formula would be 100–70 = 30 and 30 x $80,000 = $2,400,000. With the credit deduction, $2,400,000–$1,500,000 = $900,000. This is a more manageable number for a retired family with two wage earners.

Examine the situation of a single wage earner, who can exist on a 70 percent need ratio and who has enjoyed a recent annual income of $100,000, with a credit for approximately $30,000 of additional earnings or $1,000,000. If he or she retires at age sixty-five, the formula is 100–65 = 35, 35 x $70,000 = $2,450,000 and $2,450,000–$1,000,000 = $1,450,000. However, if that same individual retires at age seventy and the need ratio goes down to 65 percent, the figures become more manageable. The formula would then be 100–70 = 30; 30 x $65,000 = $1,950,000; $1,950,000–$1,000,000 = $950,000. One-half million dollars less would be required when retiring five years later.

The 5 percent reduction in the need ratio is based on the increase in Social Security benefits from ages sixty-five to seventy and additional asset returns accrued over five years.

For a professional person with a recent annual income of $200,000, retiring with a need ratio of 75 percent, requiring $150,000 ($200,000 x 75% = $150,000) per year to sustain a comparable standard of living, at age sixty-five the figures would read like this: 100–65 = 35; 35 x $150,000 = $5,250,000. Let us make a logical assumption that at this income level the retiree has amassed or perhaps inherited outside funds which, when added to government benefits, would add up to $50,000 annual income or more and justify a $2,000,000 credit deduction. The final calculation would be $5,250,000–$2,000,000 = $3,250,000. If that same person retired at age seventy, the need level would decrease to 70 percent, requiring an income of $140,000 per year. Then the calculations would be as follows: 100–70 = 30; 30 x $140,000 = $4,200,000; $4,200,000–$2,000,000 = $2,200,000. The sum is reduced by over $1,000,000 with the later retirement.

A corporate executive earning $300,000 annually is forced to take a mandatory retirement at age sixty-five. He is given a severance package which allows him to have a $3,000,000 credit deduction and reduces his need level to 67 percent, or about $200,000 a year. How much money does he require in his portfolio to enjoy a carefree retirement? Once again, 100–65 = 35; 35 x $200,000 = $7,000,000 and $7,000,000–$3,000,000 = $4,000,000. He will need to have accrued $4,000,000 in retirement savings.

If a small business owner or a surgeon, earning $500,000 in an average year, decides to sell his business or practice for a buyout price which allows him sufficient outside income of over $120,000, he is eligible for a $4,000,000 credit deduction. Using the formula, if he chooses to retire at age sixty, at a 60 percent need level or $300,000 draw per year, how much does he need to accumulate in his retirement account? 100–60 = 40.

40 x $300,000 = $12,000,000. $12,000,000–$4,000,000 credit = $8,000,000.

There are other variables which may need to be factored in, in special cases, such as unusual spending habits, abnormal expenditures, extraordinary legal fees, massive judgments or taxes to be paid, but in the norm the formula gives a general idea of what amounts are needed at various income levels.

As was made clear with the difference in the size of Social Security payments, age is a potent variable in the determination of the amount of money needed for retirement. A too-early retirement can necessitate the need for unattainable amounts of money and cause hardships later on. Another factor, which can alter the mathematics, is a windfall. If the retiring couple wishes to simplify their lives and sells or auctions off some of their collectibles and finds to their good fortune that their artworks have greatly appreciated or they sell their large house for a princely sum (or on the rare occasion of winning the lottery), these bonanzas can change the calculations. Otherwise they hold true.

UTILIZATION

Some people who will utilize the formulas on retirement monetary needs will be pleasantly surprised, if they didn't already know, that they are free from financial concern, as they have reached their goals by way of contractual agreement or by earning more than they need or desire to spend, thereby amassing large reserves.

Two retired schoolteachers, who taught in a school district with 70 percent retirement benefits, need only be concerned with how much they leave their heirs. If their combined incomes totaled about $100,000, they can easily enjoy a retirement at the same level as during their working years, periodically receiving government checks. Only if they wish to improve their standard of living by augmenting their income do they have the need for an active investment program.

In school districts or other institutions where the retirement packages are not so generous, the formulas presented apply. Another factor is certainty. Although very few governmental contracts have defaulted, in times of dire need pension plans have had to be restructured under the threat of default. So it is prudent, even in the most secure-appearing situations, to have substantial monetary reserves in case of a negative restructuring.

CHAPTER 6

Lifestyle in Anticipation of Retirement

According to a recent study, near retirees, ranging in age from sixty to sixty-four, have an average of $360,000 in all of their retirement accounts, defined contribution and IRAs combined.[6] Since this is an average, it means many have less than $360,000 saved for retirement. As was obvious from the financial formulas in the previous part of this book, $360,000 is a woefully inadequate sum for most of these soon-to-be retirees to retire at anywhere near the lifestyle they were accustomed to during their working years. Those who have much less money in their accounts may fall beneath the poverty line.

In the United States, with more and more so-called "baby boomers" coming to retirement age, the highest levels of government have become aware and even alarmed at this impending human crisis. With an increasing number of Americans already living in poverty, the last thing we need is to add to that number.

After having introduced the idea in his 2014 State of the Union address, President Obama spoke at a steel plant in western Pennsylvania about a new plan to help Americans save for retirement. The President had directed the Secretary of the Treasury to set up a government-backed individual retirement account (IRA) system linked so that employees could contribute through payroll deductions and he named this new plan MyRA. Echoing the call of the nation, Obama said, "If you've worked hard all your life, you deserve a secure retirement."

As people are living longer and the population is aging, there has to be a reassessment of the importance of the retirement period, which can approach one-third of a lifetime or more. From a retirement point of view, life can now be divided into three periods:

1. Pre-work, including infancy, childhood, puberty and adolescence, concerned with growth, schooling and preparing for a career.
2. Work, or adulthood, concerned with career progression and caring for family needs and the accumulation of adequate savings to finance the post-work years.
3. Post-work, or retirement, the senior years, where the money you have worked for now works for you.

Since the retirement period may occupy many more years of life than it did in the past, planning for it from youth should be integrated at early levels of education. Parents must become aware that it is their responsibility to be adequately prepared and wherever possible not become a burden to their children. The children must be taught, from as young an age as their understanding will allow, that they may be forced by circumstance to give up their chosen career sometime later in life and that it is important that they take on the financial responsibility to plan for that eventuality. Courses on this subject should be taught in high schools and colleges.

RESPONSIBILITY

Many Americans and people in other countries have avoided those responsibilities which were necessitated by the hardships of yesteryear. It is the price we have paid for social progress and our need for competitive affluence. Living above our means to obtain immediate desirables while neglecting our long-term needs has become commonplace. Industries have catered to our demands for excess.

Food companies exploit our excessive cravings for sweets and foods rich in fats and starches. An epidemic of obesity has plagued our young people as they emulate the gluttony of their elders. People's obsession with entertainment venues has overpowered civic responsibilities, so that television dance contests attract more voters than national elections.

Some people tend to eat what satisfies their tastebuds with little or no concern for their coronary arteries, so that heart disease is the preeminent killer in nations around the world. In many ways, a large segment of the American public have become derelict in their duty to themselves and their nation.

One of these derelictions is in not adequately preparing for future needs, not developing the discipline to save periodically when it is possible. They give in to the easy path of immediate gratification and neglect future needs. Sometimes one must say no to one's children, with a good explanation so that they are taught to understand, because financial discipline must be learned at an early age. When taught and reinforced from childhood on, this will become a lesson for a lifetime.

Even in the abundance of an affluent home, learning the value of forgoing immediate pleasure to insure the availability of something much more lasting and important later on is a valuable lesson to impart to offspring. In a middle-class home with limited resources in the current state of our economy, it should be treated as required education.

Although America is currently the richest and most powerful nation on earth, much of what we have has been achieved with borrowed money that other people have loaned us, because of our record of safety and stability. The US Treasury gives the greatest assurance of return of capital and interest available anywhere. There are powerful forces, both inside and outside our country, that are warning that America cannot continue to rely on greater and greater debt to finance the American way of life.

The preparation for each individual to be able to adequately take care of his or her retirement should be on the agenda of every family and educational organization. As with most things, education is the key. As workers age, they become anxiously aware of how little time there is left to acquire what is necessary. That is why it is vital that the teaching of what to do, how to go about it and other matters has to begin early, when it's easy to lay out a plan with plenty of time for accumulation and overcoming mistakes. The later the education takes hold and the plan is acted upon, the more difficult and painful the sacrifices will be.

Strive for self-reliance, bearing the responsibility for oneself and dependent family members throughout life, and only rely on others at times of calamitous emergencies.

In other wealthy countries around the world, benefits similar to Social Security often account for at least two-thirds of retirement income, whereas it accounts for less than half in the United States.[7] Since Americans already face these odds, it is even more important to work independently from the government in planning for retirement.

LIFE PLAN
Pre-work

The most important aspect of the pre-work phase of life, in preparation for a self-reliant retirement, is education. The more schooling you acquire in your chosen endeavor, the better entry-level position for which you will be eligible. From then on, your promotions will depend on your motivation and talent. The more you learn and the harder you work will determine the level of your success and the subsequent monetary reward. Studies have shown that, on average, the higher the degree of education attained, the higher the salary. High school graduates make more money than drop-outs and college graduates make more money than high school graduates. Attaining a graduate degree in a given field usually equates to a greater monetary reward.

Besides the occasional story of some genius billionaire who made his fortune after dropping out of school, most dropouts do poorly. Staying in school and getting as far as your brain and desire will let you is of paramount importance for earning the maximum you can. The more you earn, the more goods and services you can acquire, but this also tests the necessary discipline required to save and invest for your future. The earlier you begin to put a portion of your income aside for retirement, the less that portion need be.

Work

The true test of financial discipline occurs when you begin to earn good money and it comes time for you to determine how much to put into a defined contribution plan, such as an employer-sponsored payroll deduction 401(k) plan and/or an IRA. A typical table of the percentage of earnings required for the various periods of distribution needs shows how much more you require the later you start:

When Started	Percent Needed to Reach Goals
Early: During first 5 years of employment	10%–12%
Middle: During 5–10 years of employment	12%–15%
Late: During 10–20 years of employment	15%–20%
Very Late: Over 20 years of employment	25%–40%

It is readily discernible that in an average work life of thirty-five to forty years, if one has not begun to contribute heavily to a retirement plan before the later stages of employment, draconian saving measures are required to play catchup, at a time of life when added expenses, such as children's college tuition payments, pile up. This may be an added factor, besides the obvious one of insufficient funds in general, as to why so many students are saddled with large student loans and come out of school heavily in debt.

NON-WORK FACTORS DURING WORK YEARS
Debt

All debts, including business loans, student loans, personal loans, credit card debt, car loans, mortgages, liens, alimony, child support and others should be satisfied before retirement, paid up or easily payable without affecting any other calculable aspects. All retirement formula calculations in this book have assumed a relatively debt-free situation.

Business

One of the most desirable ways to retire is by passing an ongoing business to heirs or partners with a continuing stream of income coming in, which will nicely take care of the retiree and his or her dependents. Whether it's a small family business with the children carrying on or a generous severance package from a mid-size company, guaranteed financial security to insure a comfortable retirement necessitates only supplemental investing. These people usually don't need my formulas. However, their guarantees are only as strong as the companies which issue them and companies, even large and prosperous ones, sometimes fail. It is imperative that even the most secure retirement packages should be backed up by sufficient personal wealth to carry on in case of severe business setbacks.

Those of more modest means who venture into the business world must always protect themselves from failure. Businesses should be incorporated to limit personal liability. One of the most crippling roadblocks to a retirement plan is personal bankruptcy, with creditors clamoring for payment and credit compromised. Before becoming a first-time entrepreneur, one should be fully prepared managerially, besides being technically proficient in the craft of the enterprise. If you don't have a business degree or experience, read up on it and get advice from professionals. Consult your lawyer, if you have one, your banker and/or your accountant. If you don't have one of these, get one. You will need all of them sooner or later if you continue with the venture.

Each year thousands of inexperienced people with bright ideas and a modicum of expertise in their field try to establish businesses. Many of them fail, not because they are poor workers, although some might be, but because they lack sufficient capital to adequately finance what they are trying to do. Or, if they do raise enough money, they budget poorly and overspend. It is not the lack of technical expertise that dooms them as much as it is their lack of managerial skills. Before going into business, consult with experienced professionals in allied and other industries to discuss the viability of your business plan. Find out ahead of time how much money you will need and how to spend those funds efficiently. Do the research. Choose the proposed business site with care. Check out your competition. Be sure there is a market for your product. Investigate your backers so you know who you are dealing with. Do not trust to chance. Be careful: this might be the only time in your life that you will have the opportunity to be your own boss.

Come to know yourself. Are you one who wants to be out on his own, taking responsibility, making the final decisions, or are you more comfortable letting others lead the way? Do you want to be the boss, telling others what to do, or would you rather someone else told you what to do? Would you rather be one of a crowd or be at the head of the pack? Are you destined to be an employer or an employee? Many people don't know what role is in their future until they have experience in their field. To some the road is clear and the choice obvious from the beginning. Some start out as employees, find contentment in their work and stay that way for a lifetime. Others, after gaining experience in their field, are frustrated at not being able to have the freedom of autonomy and thus go out on their own.

There is much to be said about being one's own boss. There are many people who just can't work happily for others. They want things done their way. They need the freedom to express themselves, to put their stamp on their little part of the world. They are convinced that it is their destiny to lead and not to follow. In part, leadership is inspiration and talent, but to succeed it takes motivation and hard work. It is a mental phenomenon, conceived in ideation and carried out in devotion. Not all are capable of achieving, or even desiring, this responsibility and this has left many people all over the world with a grave problem.

The United States of America was founded by men with what today is considered to be a "small business" mentality. George Washington was a farmer, Thomas Jefferson and John Adams were lawyers, Benjamin Franklin was a printer, Benjamin Rush was a doctor and so on. Differing from the peasant revolutions in France and Russia, which were wars against their aristocracies, the American Revolution was an uprising of men of financial substance against a perceived oppressive foreign monarchy. This war was fought to free us from taxation without representation and to stop America from being a controlled colony. These independent men wanted to establish in the Northern Hemisphere of the New World a nation free of the constraints of the social, political and religious prejudices that plagued eighteenth century Europe, a nation that allowed anyone, no matter how lowborn, to be able to rise up and achieve whatever his talent and desire could attain.

Subsequently, America became a nation of small business people. As these businesses grew, employees were hired. Often the menial jobs were taken by newly-arrived immigrants. Gradually, ambitious men with innovative ideas grew these small businesses into larger ones requiring more and more employees. Many of the new immigrants, who had a history of self-employment in their native lands as farmers, grocers, merchants and doctors and had escaped persecution elsewhere, could not or would not gain even entry-level status in another's employ and thus started out on their own. Whether plowing the fields of a land grant in the West or peddling from a pushcart in the East, America spawned generation after generation of entrepreneurs. Overcoming many hardships, these pioneers became self-sufficient.

As big businesses grew larger and larger and were joined in evolving industries with other big businesses, the ratio of workers to bosses grew to the point that a nation conceived of by small businessmen became a nation mostly of working men and women. The Industrial Revolution of the latter part of the nineteenth century created an additional demand for workers with various skills. World War II propelled the United States into world leadership and new industries developed as a result of wartime research and development. For the average individual, the impetus was no longer to start a new business—it was to get a job in someone else's business.

As businesses grew larger, small businesses were bought out or simply made obsolete. Unless one was endowed with great technical expertise, a very keen mind, lacked familial responsibilities and had great courage and access to financing, it became more and more difficult to compete against established companies. Even well-educated students from fine schools became imbued with the concept that after graduation they would seek out high-paying jobs with good benefits.

As the economies of other nations began to emerge, their cheap labor attracted businesses seeking larger profits to gratify their stockholders. Little by little, manufacturing jobs moved to the teeming workshops of other countries. Positions which had been traditionally available to unskilled Americans disappeared. Factories, like those of the clothing industry, were transported abroad. Jobs began to become more scarce.

Then, perhaps for the first time in the history of commerce, great innovation, instead of increasing the demand for a larger workforce, caused a loss of jobs. The technological revolution of the last decade of the twentieth century and on into the early twenty-first has caused people to be replaced by machines. Although highly-skilled workers are still desired and sought after, those not so skilled are hard pressed to find work. Many middle-aged workers have been laid off and, even if they do find work, they are underemployed at low-paying jobs below their skill levels. Entry-level jobs are hard to find, so many recent graduates can't find work and we now have a generation facing the unpleasant situation of having to move back in with their parents. This dependency and financial strain on the previous generation will certainly disrupt many retirement plans.

Another factor inhibiting America from becoming a start-up nation again (a country with a large number of brand new businesses) is the matter of available financing. Although the Federal Reserve has made money readily available for lending by keeping interest rates low, due to the recent severe recession banks are reluctant to make under-secured loans. Therefore, many aspiring entrepreneurs have to get by on unemployment benefits while awaiting alternate financing.

A small nation like Israel, which has the most per capita start-up businesses in the world, has one of the lowest percentages of unemployment among developed countries. It has also been advocated that entrepreneurial skills are honed in the military. Advanced technological knowledge and leadership skills acquired during military training should allow our returning veterans to engage in new ventures, if the government is wise enough to endorse adequate programs to make financing available. Veterans deserve this and our country needs it. Many veterans are returning from lengthy service abroad and are faced with an uncertain job market. We have to stop being mainly a country of employees. We must regain the vitality to become a nation of innovators and employers.

ADULT EDUCATION

Concerned people are horrified by news broadcasts of the violence in our schools. Bullying has been going on for a long time, but shootings and killings appear to have escalated during recent years. Whether this is the result of the greater availability of firearms or of more widespread reporting by the media is for the statisticians to decide. What cannot be denied is that our schools have been subjected to another influence besides education. It is a well-known fact that the immature years are times of greater physicality than the mature ones and this drive for physical expression was expected to be healthfully dissipated in competitive athletics. Unfortunately, the athletic programs available were insufficient to quell the anger and penchant for violence fostered by negative home and environmental influences. The street and schoolyard mentality has been brought into the classroom. Disrespect for teachers and class disruption have become all too commonplace. In some schools, the loss of disciplinary control has gone so far that it has resulted in student and teacher intimidation and violence. Students who want to learn are being deterred and distracted from learning out of fear for their safety and, in some cases, their very lives.

Added to the school shootings reported to be occurring at the elementary and secondary school levels are the many reports of college campus rapes and sexual assaults in the military services. It appears that a segment of our educational institutions has become a breeding ground for violence.

For some years there have existed in some countries groups of poor and deprived and therefore angry people with an anti-educational counter-culture, a counter-culture which has denigrated educational striving, a culture which has resulted in neglect of learning, failing grades, truancy, expulsions and ultimately poor preparation for the workplace. Many who might have had the ability to learn and advance were influenced by peer pressure to neglect their studies and abandoned what could have been bright futures for a life of menial work or, even worse, a life of crime. Some of these poor students had no choice: the poverty about them demanded that they leave school to find work to help their families. Others just didn't have the intelligence to learn beyond what they did. Many just didn't take advantage of the educational opportunities available to them.

As we are currently faced with worldwide unemployment woes, many people from many lands are clamoring to come to America to compete for the skilled jobs that are not able to be filled by Americans, who have not acquired the needed skills. It then is the responsibility of those who did not take advantage of the opportunities given them as young people to avail themselves of whatever retraining programs are available for them today.

No one should be overwhelmed by the prospect of adult education. Everyone can learn. Life experiences, in some cases, actually make it easier to be a better student in adulthood.

A great challenge is the restructuring of the educational system to accommodate the demands of the modern workplace.

Nineteenth century models of education no longer work. There is more to learn than ever before and college tuitions are less affordable than ever before. The educational process should be streamlined and compacted to eliminate the unusable and retain and add usable courses tailor-made for each curriculum.

FAMILY

The year I was born, 1933, was the height of the Great Depression. The unemployment rate reached nearly 25 percent. With one out of four eligible workers out of work, the newly elected administration enacted much supportive legislation under a New Deal for the American public. The poor and infirmed could now count on public funds in times of need. As some wage earners could not get readily reintroduced into the workforce, this public assistance became a way of life for numerous families. In many cases, it was advantageous for the primary wage earner not to be present for the funds to continue coming in. This near, or actual, poverty-level existence often led to family disruption. Many men, unable to provide for their families, abandoned them. Others, not being able to support a family, sired children out of wedlock and left. Vices associated with poverty erupted. Incidents of alcoholism, gambling, drug dealing and abuse, robberies, burglaries, rapes and murders began to grow in number. Single-teenage-mother families became numerous rather than an oddity.

Despite the post-war boom, in some American cities there were men, initiated into a public assistance habituation, who did not return to the workforce. Some single parents passed on this cultural heritage of the paternalistic benevolence of government in the form of public assistance to their children. With the understanding of schooling as a pre-work endeavor, since work was no longer to be strived for, neither was learning. Thus the counter-culture spread.

The United States of America, a relatively young country created through the toil of its inhabitants, inadvertently spawned an expensive and anti-productive counter-culture which has resulted, in some ways, in producing many non-skilled individuals who are ill-equipped to compete in the twenty-first century job market for high-paying jobs. However, this wasn't the only reason for an ill-prepared workforce. Many well-educated students became proficient in areas where there no longer was sufficient demand for the number of applicants for new jobs in those fields. Studies have shown that family influence is paramount in motivating a child to develop the discipline and respect required to succeed in school and at work.

President Barack Obama and I have something in common. We both grew up under the major influence of one parent. My father died when I was fourteen and I am proud to say I owe everything I have achieved to my mother, an immigrant seamstress who intoned over and over again to her only son, "Stay in school and make something of yourself."

One of the best ways to show your love for your children is to imbue them with a love of learning and a striving for success. This is a competitive world; giving your children the motivation to strive to be the best that they can be at everything they want to do is a parent's sacred duty.

LOVE

What you will read in this section on love and the following sections on marriage and divorce was gleaned from the many years I have spent treating patients in family therapy. I was one of the first members of the American Academy of Clinical Sexologists. I became certified in sex counseling, was a contributing editor to a magazine devoted to medical sexology and subsequently became a Fellow of the American Academy of Clinical Sexologists.

Love is a complex and misunderstood emotion. Many misinterpret lust for love. Others try to turn like into love. We notice this in the misuse of the word itself. We speak of loving a food, an article of clothing, a piece of furniture or just about anything we like a lot. We speak of loving so many things (and in some cases, people) that love is undoubtedly one of the most overused words in the English language.

As we explore all the things that influence life from the perspective of retirement comfort being the ultimate goal, we have to assume that the love(s) of the individual will have a considerable bearing on the process.

There are different levels of true love. Love has been described as giving away a part of yourself to someone else and loving that part as much as the rest of yourself that's left behind. The purest example of this kind of love is the love of a parent for a child, because the parent doesn't have to give anything additional away, since the child already has a part of the parent in his or her DNA. Because of acquired mannerisms, many parents see a part of themselves in their children and they love them like life itself and would sacrifice anything for them.

The love between lovers has the additional quality of sexual attraction. Only if accompanied by emotional caring, the feeling that you would give up your life to save this person, can this combination be called true love. Emotional caring is by far the more subtle of the two feelings and sometimes takes much longer to develop. Sexual attraction is a more spectacular sensation, caused by the thrill induced through hormonal chemistry. Sexual attraction excites the passion that entices the poet to write poems and the songwriter to compose love songs. While attraction is a roaring fire which may be extinguished with time, emotional caring is a smoldering ember which holds its spark over the years. Real love must have both components to last. Unfortunately many people, attracted and enticed by media over-evaluation of sexual importance in relationships, fall in love with being in love. Attainment of that certain feeling, that blending of chemistry, leads to the belief that sex is love.

In some ways we may consider sexual attraction to be the immature component, since it is innate and comes naturally, usually first encountered in adolescence. We all remember our first love or crush. The hormonal explosion of the teen years led to sexual exploration and being overwhelmed by feelings. This hyper-emotionality leads to an over-evaluation of the importance of our feelings, pushing us to make rash decisions which could affect a lifetime, without the wisdom of experience.

Many who act on the impulse of the chemical reactions of the immature body without following more mature advice come to regret this later on. What is experienced as true love is a beautiful thing, but the mere sexual substitute gone wrong can be a derailment for future plans.

The capacity for emotional caring, the mature component of love, comes later in life. It requires a knowledge of self that only comes with interpersonal experience. You have to learn what is important to you and what isn't, what you like in a close relationship and what you don't, what turns you on and what turns you off, what qualities are needed for a soul mate. A definite level of maturity is needed to be able to really commit to a true love relationship.

MARRIAGE

Years ago, when the average lifespan was forty or so years, marriage was a simple affair. You finished your schooling, went to work, got married, had kids and worked until you died. Since we live twice as long as people used to, marriage is now more complicated. Where it had been a relatively short-term decision on who to marry, now it's a long-term decision. We have become accustomed to short-term relationships with many things. It used to be that craftsmen had pride in their work and it was an attribute to make things that lasted. When the "bean counters" took control of industrial production, they found that making things that last meant that the consumers would not buy new ones for a long time and that was bad for profits. So the manufacturers began to produce items that would only function for a limited period ("planned obsolescence") so people would buy replacements. In the technological age, the turnover went from years to months.

This culture of rapid exchange has translated from things to people. With the greater mobility of the population and the travel demands of the workplace, many who in olden times would have kept friends for a lifetime now have to re-acclimate periodically to new environments. The need for permanence, once prized, is no longer vital. If a better job is available many miles away, we tend to move. Upward mobility within a company is the road to advancement and a bigger paycheck. The move is made, sometimes at the expense of familial disruption and marital failure. Having more than one spouse in a lifetime, once a rarity, is now commonplace.

Psychologically there are two types of marriages, hormonal and compatible. The hormonal relationship is based on a great love affair and often both parties would have been better off if it had remained that way and run its course. The great physical attraction can overcome the problems that invariably arise in some cases, but often it is replaced by a physical attraction to someone else. This happens because the hormonal relationship, at its core, is immature, shallow and fickle. While opposites attract, similarities last. A great physical attraction without a great similarity of interests and desires leaves no grounding of emotional support to overcome the lust of the next physical attraction.

The compatibility marriage usually occurs with more mature people, often in those who were previously hurt by a hormonal relationship at a younger age. As the couple has matured, the adventure is less dramatic and proceeds from friendship.

More than half of American marriages end as broken contracts as they do not continue to fulfill the vow, "until death do us part." That may not be the whole story. In my experience I have observed that two out of three hormonal marriages tend to fail, while only one out of three compatibility marriages end earlier than intended. The institution of marriage remains a fifty/fifty proposition for all marriages but you have twice the chance of remaining married for a lifetime if you marry later in life, based on a strong friendship rather than just on chemistry. Sparks, butterflies in the stomach and bells ringing are great for love affairs, but they do not sustain over the course of financial woes, children keeping you up through the night and dirty dishes in the sink.

If you want it all—the romance, the magic and the final stability to sustain you in later life—then satisfy your hormonal urges without commitment until you are mature enough, experienced enough and self-aware enough to make the correct final choice. With the expertise of someone who has been married for over fifty years to the same spouse, I can tell you that the pleasure of being with someone who is a willing teammate, a true friend and partner, a great parent and grandparent, someone who loves you for who you are and doesn't need or want to change you, is worth the wait.

CHILDREN

When we were an agricultural society, children were not only a blessing but an asset. A son could help work the fields and do the farm chores and a daughter could help her mother do the housework and lend a hand in the kitchen. The more children one had, the more that would get done and more efficiently. Today, this is generally no longer true. Outside infrequent cases where children care for an indigent parent, children have become increasingly expensive to raise and even more expensive to educate.

I will never forget an experience that I had years ago. I had been called to come to a psychiatric hospital where I was on staff late at night to admit a suicidal patient of mine, who had been brought in as an emergency. When I was through interviewing the patient and the family members who came with her and finished the required paperwork, I left to go to my car. It was now past midnight. In the hospital parking lot I ran into an old colleague, a refined gentleman in his early seventies. I asked him what he was doing at the hospital so late at night and he told me that he had to schedule so many patients during the day he could only make hospital rounds late at night, and that he worked every work night until midnight or so. When I asked him why he was pushing himself so hard at an age when other psychiatrists were usually cutting back their caseloads, he told me he had twelve children and the two youngest were still in medical school, so he had tuitions to pay. When I asked him if he ever planned to retire, he just laughed. Within two years he was dead. He worked until his heart gave out. I swore soon after that I would never have a similar fate.

If, like my late colleague, you feel it your responsibility as a parent to pay for the education of your children, even if they go on to graduate-level education, you are assuming a sizeable financial burden. If you cherish your children, as most parents do, and can readily afford this, fine, but if you would assume debt instead of allowing your children to go out into the workplace laden with their own debt, delaying your retirement may be the price you will have to pay for doing so.

Besides the normal costs of raising children, let us just calculate the tuition costs per child. Good private schools are now charging $50,000 and up per year. Unless you are raising a gifted athlete or can show sufficient need for a scholarship, your son or daughter will cost you $200,000 plus room and board if they live away from home, or a quarter of a million dollars per child. If they decide to study medicine or go into some other graduate program, you might have to double that figure. Many middle-income children will have to be content with going to community colleges and enrolling in two-year programs, or enrolling in online schools while they work—if they can find work. Those who can't find jobs may have to come back home and will need financial support. Many parents wouldn't have the heart to deny a gifted child the best educational opportunity available and would gladly sacrifice for them, but with large families it would be inconceivable.

From a strictly financial perspective as middle-class parents, I feel it is best to limit the number of children you have to two or three. Debt owed on student loans is enormous, with the constant threat of increasing pressure to pay off these overdue loans. The trade-off is having fewer children you can afford to treat well versus having the blessing of a large family which you might not be able to care for in the manner you would like. This is an individual choice, but from the point of view of retirement planning, a smaller family is the way to go.

DIVORCE

Over the past century, a major cultural shift occurred. For many, marriage is no longer a lifetime commitment. Women as well as men have the right to claim that they no longer want to be married to their current spouses. A new age has dawned, an age of change, an age of only temporary alignment, of temporary love, of widespread sexual experimentation. Satisfying the needs of another in a continuing union, to many, is a thing of the past. Many now forsake marital commitment and merely cohabitate to avoid the downside of divorce.

Divorce laws and attorneys have turned the divorce process into an impending nightmare for many. We live in an age of great sexual freedom. Many involved parents no longer counsel abstinence; they caution the use of condoms. The increase in the number of sexual relationships during the pre-marital years has contributed to the relegation of temporary status in relationships. The increase in the number of divorces is a product of people not wanting to attempt to work out what has gone wrong with a marriage, but rather to attempt to find out what could be better with a new relationship. In cases of extreme cruelty and abuse, there is no argument: the relationship should be terminated. However, in many other cases, much less severe differences can be overcome with proper professional help. In a culture that today says divorce is okay, marriage is a more fragile and temporary institution than ever before.

There are those individuals who are perpetual losers. As a group they appear to be fixated with an immature attitude toward the nature of who they are, what they want and what to expect from another person in a close relationship. I had a friend, a family physician, who complained to me about his third wife. He had finally attained the insight to realize that he had basically married the same woman three times. The same complaints he had about the third one applied to the first two. They even looked alike. My friend had an immature approach to choosing a wife. When he finally realized his mistake, it was too late, because he already had child support and forthcoming school costs to consider and his dream home in Florida was not to be realized. He was never able to retire.

Although matters like sexual incompatibility, dissimilarities in interests and fights over childrearing are factors that drive couples apart, most arguments between husbands and wives are over money. The lack of the availability of adequate funds to satisfy the needs and desires of a family is a major deterrent to a harmonious relationship between spouses. When the basic expectations of a spouse are not met, disappointment turns into frustration and resentment. Comparisons are made to other people's more affluent situations and other opportunities that were available that could have brought better living conditions. Lack of money for household requirements tests the strength of every relationship. It takes frugality, caring and a strong commitment to the marriage by people who are mature enough to see that what they do have is more important than what they don't have. It is very difficult to live through a period of want and many marriages are not strong enough, nor the partnership mature enough, to survive it. Yet many do and actually survive in larger numbers than more affluent marriages where divorce promises greater rewards than when there is little to haggle over.

Whereas immaturity in commitment is the major cause for marital failure, in my experience the greatest cause for estrangement is disagreement over the allocation of the available money. In either case, divorce is one of the greatest obstacles in the way of a successful retirement.

Although most children are resilient, divorce affects them all and can take a lasting psychological toll on the most sensitive ones. Strongly antagonistic divorces, with combative recriminations, may leave long-term mental scars. The children's well-being should always be discussed when contemplating separation. In my experience it is wisest to gradually acclimate them to their two parents living apart, rather than wait until the last minute and shock them. It is often wisest for a child to face a personal tragedy in increments, whenever this is possible, rather than to face it all at once.

No matter how bleak the future of a marriage seems to one or both of the partners, I strongly advise professional counseling to seek amiable solutions. In my own practice, many couples who felt their marriages were no longer viable benefitted from a new and nonjudgmental approach offered in therapy. Being able to step back and reassess the problems from a new perspective, in a calm environment, can often lead to an understanding of how to move forward in a different direction. The process is not perfect—some marriages are just too damaged to save—but it is always incumbent on two people, who at one time felt so strongly attached to each other to get married, to try to recapture what they once had, if not for selfish reasons, then to spare their children from the trauma of familial disruption. It is the parents' duty to try to shield the children from as many unpleasant experiences as possible; avoiding a costly and traumatizing divorce process ranks high on that list.

CRIME

Having a criminal record can be a retirement killer. Public officials who are found guilty of graft or corruption are often stripped of their pensions. Those who have self-directed retirement plans, if they have to serve a sentence for any length of time, may lose their jobs and find few employers are willing to hire someone with a prison record.

The smartest of criminals get caught. Talking yourself into or allowing someone else to convince you that you will be the exception and escape detection is a fool's errand. Just about all get-rich-quick schemes fail. Most professional endeavors are measured by percentages. A medication or medical procedure has to be proven effective in a reasonable percentage of trial subjects before gaining approval from the regulatory agencies for widespread public use. When the drug or modality only succeeds in a small percentage of trial patients it is discarded. To try to get a large sum through some illegal maneuver is a very high-risk adventure, with little chance of succeeding. No matter the circumstance, doing something against the law is a bad move. Discard the thought; wave off the temptation as too risky. Get away from those who would lead you astray.

The size of the legal fees of criminal defense teams alone should deter anyone from contemplating a criminal act. Imagine shelling out up to $1000 an hour. Any intensive legal involvement, unless it's through a public defender, pro bono or on a contingency basis, can be financially crippling. Legal fees have brought down many wealthy people, let alone an ordinary citizen. Before you act to deprive anyone else of something of value for your own benefit, remember how the odds are stacked against you and don't do it. The ultimate loss may be far greater than the gain imagined. Think of your legacy: Do you want your children to grow up with the image of their parent as a thief? How would you feel if they had to visit you while you were incarcerated?

ADDICTIONS

Prolonged addictions to drugs, alcohol or gambling are potential retirement destroyers. The cost of a narcotic or gambling addiction can deplete any bankroll. The employment time lost due to alcoholism can cause job loss and long periods of unemployment. Even if treatment is sought, the time and cost of inpatient rehabilitation will be a drain.

Because of this widespread problem, some companies have beneficial allowances for treatment time for valued employees. Still, the cost due to work hours that have been lost because of addictions is considerable.

One effective form of therapy seems to be group therapy, like the Anonymous programs for alcohol (AA), gambling (GA) and narcotics (NA). They teach step-based curricula for abstinence through day-by-day vigilance and supervision by a seasoned, sober sponsor. Still, there are too many who relapse and have to start anew. There are also now programs for families of addicts, like Al-Anon, to help them to better understand the struggle their loved ones are going through and to be in a position to lend support.

I have personally witnessed medical careers destroyed by addictions which grew so expensive to support that the physicians had to become illegal drug dispensers to afford to pay for their habits. These compromised doctors had to face the shame and embarrassment of chastisement by disciplinary medical boards and the disgrace of the resulting suspension of their licenses to practice medicine. Some had to relocate to other states in the hope of being reinstated, while others had to quit the profession altogether. Five to eight years of graduate study and the sacrifice for a professional career and its benefits had gone to waste. *Addicted Healers: 5 Key Signs Your Healthcare Professional May Be Drug Impaired* by Ethan O. Bryson, MD, delves into the hidden world of medical professionals addicted to prescription drugs.

CHAPTER 7

Affluent Behavior Patterns

In the final analysis, preparation for retirement centers on the accumulation of sufficient money to finance a comfortable retirement lifestyle. According to the formulas in this book, the amount required at most earning levels is in excess of one million dollars. To formulate a prerequisite lifestyle which would teach us what we actually have to do to facilitate the accumulation of such an amount of money, we should refer to studies which have analyzed the behavior patterns of millionaires. The millionaires we are referring to are not members on a list of the richest people in the world. They are mostly self-made small businessmen, professionals and company employees who, through a pattern of living, have been able to amass enough money to meet the formula criteria for retirement.

Here is a list of the financial behavior patterns of these affluent individuals:

1. They tend to live a lifestyle conducive to accumulating money.

They do not spend much of their money on things that depreciate, but reserve their purchases for things that appreciate. So they would rather purchase a work of art that will go up in value than a yacht of the same cost, which most likely will sell for considerably less than the original purchase price. They value and respect money and budget carefully, knowing where their money goes. They tend to be organized. When buying an automobile, they consult the rating agencies and buy the highest-rated car for safety and reliability within their price range and are careful not to overpay. They negotiate from a position of having done the research to know what the price should be. Whenever making an important acquisition, they know what they are prepared to spend and they do not binge shop or buy things they will never use. If they really want an extravagant gift or indulgence, they set aside a special savings plan to grow the needed funds. As a rule they are a harmonious family with a singular purpose toward financial security and they impart this value to their children.[8]

2. They live well below their means.

This appears to be the element most essential to accumulating wealth. If at a young age you can learn to give up the quest for instant gratification and learn to plan for the long term, this lesson will sustain you for a lifetime. This financial discipline is the basis for not trying to outwit trends and to stay the long course in investing, as the long course has always surged upward. The affluent tend to put aside a much larger part of their income in savings as compared to the population as a whole. This is a type of financial maturity. The immature teenager is often enticed by passing fads and wants to spend unwisely on items that will soon be discarded. If this attitude is carried into adulthood, with happiness being equated with accumulating luxurious things at the expense of preparing for a secure future, retirement requirements will not be met.

Many fortunes have been squandered because of immature overindulgence. We read with dismay about professional athletes, usually coming from impoverished backgrounds, who are suddenly thrust into the public spotlight at a young age, with lucrative contracts and the trimmings of instant celebrity. Many attempt to overcome their own insecurities with a show of lavish extravagance. They live by the misconception that to show how successful you are you have to throw money around. It's okay if you are also saving a big enough chunk to support yourself after your playing days are over, but if not, then it is foolish. Many who earn millions, because of spending for the present while ignoring the needs of the future, wind up broke in the end.

Those of us who have been poor at some time in our lives know what deprivation means and try to avoid the return of that hateful status, sometimes by spending very sparingly. When you are young and poor and you live in a neighborhood where all your friends are also poor, you don't mind being poor as much. However, if you have lived better and had the taste of a finer life and then have to relinquish it, the sense of disappointment can be overwhelming. In therapy sessions, I have experienced the anguish of those who foolishly believed the good times would never end and didn't put enough away for the days of modest earnings that followed.

I had a watershed moment in regard to this topic. After my father died, my mother and I had to exist on her meager salary as a seamstress. I earned what I could as a delivery boy for the local pharmacy. On the rare occasion we could afford to eat at a restaurant it was with the understanding we would order from the right side of the menu, where the prices were, not the left side. We had to eat not what we wanted most, but what we could afford. My mother was a shrewd money manager of the tiny amount she made and this is how she kept us from going broke and paid the rent. Her best friend was the butcher's wife and so we bought meat at a price we could afford. After I finished my internship, I became a partner with a surgeon in a family medical practice. The night after my first week in practice, my partner and I went out to a pricy restaurant to celebrate the first week of our partnership. For the first time in my life,

I was able to order whatever I wanted from the menu. If you respect the significance of moments like these, you don't ever want to put yourself back into the situation to have to relive times of deprivation. You count your blessings and make sure they will keep coming. You don't throw caution to the wind and spend extravagantly to satisfy immature cravings. You maintain your focus on your future.

More than any one thing that separates those who have more than enough from those who wind up with less than they need is the fact that they tend to live below their means. In a middle-class existence, giving in to a midlife crisis and indulging in an unaffordable sports car or mistress can lead to dire consequences. Those who balance their income against outflow with an eye on the future ultimately reap the reward of secure contentment at life's end. If you are sure you can easily afford it, by all means indulge whatever your heart desires, but if you are not sure, proceed with caution. Those who are affluent usually do.[9]

3. They allocate not only their money, but their time and their energy efficiently in ways conducive to building wealth.

They consider the production of wealth a necessary endeavor and are continually learning new ways to increase their fortune. They allocate their assets appropriately to maximize both growth and income. They follow the markets they are invested in, be it stock, bond, real estate or commodities, closely. They know what's happening internationally and keep up with the news during the course of each day. They are actively involved in decisions concerning the management of their wealth. If they hire a money manager, they do so with caution after careful research. They check up on references and schedule periodic progress evaluations. They are never too busy, no matter what their other obligations are, to take the time required to be aware of where their money is and how it's doing. Even though it may be hard to earn money, it can be even harder to keep it and harder still to make it grow. It takes an appreciation of the importance of growth and the ease of loss. It takes learning to become sophisticated enough not to fall for unsafe schemes and deceptions.

Earning money takes work. So does keeping it growing and safe. Those who work hard for their money are usually devastated when it is somehow lost. The loss is of less impact when the money is gotten through an unexpected windfall and then readily dispersed, leaving the recipient no worse off than before. Studies of people who win fortunes at games of chance, gambling, lotteries and the like show that many are stripped of their fortunes almost as quickly as they acquire them. Easy come, easy go. Most gamblers lose: Las Vegas is synonymous with lost wages. Consistent winners typically don't gamble with anything more than disposable income. Those who value the importance of financial independence don't gamble with any important sums. They may take calculated risks, but they always know and respect the odds.[10]

4. They believe that financial independence is more important than displaying their social status.

They tend to regard their own inner feelings and the well-being of their loved ones above what their neighbors and the outside world think of them. There are many tales about unwise people overspending to impress others, only to find themselves in ruin. Usually these people are insecure in what they think of themselves, so they have to attempt to buy praise from others. You know who they are: the guy who can barely make his mortgage payments but insists on buying a round of drinks for everyone in the bar. The person who hasn't had a raise in years yet outbids everyone for an antique at an auction. The woman who must wear the latest fashions while struggling to pay rent. The ones who always say, "Might as well spend it now, you can't take it with you," often wind up leaving their heirs with a funeral bill and nothing else.

All that really matters, in my opinion, is family. Many people who chase fame and the approval of others find this out too late. What the world thinks of you pales in comparison to what you think of yourself. If the world loves you and you hate yourself, all you feel is depression and despair. When it seems like the world hates and despises you but you love yourself, you still retain the hope that things will get better. Living to please others and gain their admiration only works if you are trying to butter up your boss. Status doesn't mean much when your checks bounce. Making peace with yourself means putting the wants of your family first and being able to meet their needs, while you are alive and even beyond, before trying to impress others. The world may soon forget you, but your family never will.

The lesson to be learned from studying the life patterns of those who exceed their monetary goals is the importance of foregoing the appearance of wealth in order to accumulate real wealth. The appearance and perception of wealth may be trappings required in some business ventures, but in personal matters these are just superficial façades when not backed up by hard cash. Learning and applying these principles at a young age and teaching them to your children is vital to fully understanding what is really important in planning for retirement.[11]

5. Most of those studied appeared not to have had much inherited wealth, but were basically self-made.

What they did have was common sense about business matters and a strong desire to succeed. Collectively, they appeared to appreciate that we basically exist in what has been called a "boom-or-bust economy," wherein there are fluctuations between highs and lows, but with a continuous bias to the upside. Over the long term, our free enterprise system promotes growth and prosperity; hard work, careful planning and adhering to the plan usually pay off.

They appear to have compensated for what their parents didn't or couldn't give them by achieving on their own. In the spirit of the promise of their dream lives, they took on the challenge to outdo the previous generation, to have it better than those who came before them. They exemplify the statement that the American dream is still alive and well, that if you work hard and handle your finances prudently, you will succeed in building a cash reserve adequate to sustain you throughout your lifetime.[12]

6. Their adult children are economically self-sufficient.

Throughout the world we are seeing a growing disparity between the relatively affluent and the lower economic classes. Comparing the super-rich to the rest of the population in some countries, the gaps are disturbing. While much has been made about the growing difference between the haves and have-nots in the United States, our situation pales against statistics that are coming from former socialist countries. The fifty richest people in the United States have been reported to have 4 percent of the personal wealth of the nation. In Russia, the fifty wealthiest control 40 percent of the wealth. In the impoverished country of Ukraine, the fifty richest oligarchs own almost half of the personal wealth. A United Nations report indicated that the richest 1 percent of adults in the world own 40 percent of the planet's wealth.[13] In autocratically-governed countries around the world the numbers may be even more lopsided. The economical configuration depicted as a pyramid shows it swaying on an ever narrowing tip. This tipping over is seen in the many antigovernment revolts during the past several years. Graft and corruption are rampant on an enormous scale around the world. We are experiencing the plunder of the wealth of nations in amounts never before conceived of. Even in areas where wealth is usually felt to be scrutinized closely, to assure that it was acquired legitimately, the number of billionaires is growing annually and the frustration of the disenfranchised is growing daily.

There have been studies done to find out why the divide between the upper-middle class in the United States and the lower economical classes is persisting and even growing larger. With the workplace often no longer a nine-to-five affair, many people with tight schedules are only exposed to fellow workers. Normally these coworkers have things in common, with common goals, and are therefore attracted to each other. We find more lawyers marrying lawyers and more doctors marrying doctors and other rich professionals. With the greater demands of the workplace and less time to meet people outside of work, the only social interaction available to many workers is with people in the same industry. Since similar level workers, executives and professionals within each industry tend to have similar educational backgrounds and mutual interests, it stands to reason there would be a natural basis for attraction. Thus the highly educated are marrying among themselves and wealth is marrying wealth.

This increasing marriage of the well-educated leads to having children who are brought up to understand that a college education and a probable graduate level education are in their future. Parental pressure is brought to bear, in varying degrees, to get good grades so that entrance into the workforce will be easier and at a higher entrance level. The cycle continues, with wealth perpetuating wealth.

Having adult children who are economically self-sufficient lifts a great burden from the shoulders of a potential retiree. Having to support adult dependents can be very expensive and often causes resentment and familial disharmony. Not only for the benefit of the children, but for good retirement planning, make sure your children get a good education or technical training so that they will not put a strain on your retirement budget when they grow up.

We live in a world that has seen steadily inflating prices. An automobile that cost $10,000 thirty or forty years ago is $50,000 today. The price of a house, even in a recession, is still many times greater than twenty or so years ago. Clothes, furniture, appliances and other commodities are more expensive than in years gone by. Due to this inflationary trend it is important for your children to earn more than you do, because almost everything they will buy will cost more. Therefore, giving your children every opportunity to be self-sufficient even beyond your own level of success is really important not only for their success, but for your own future needs in retirement.

Responsibility should start to be taught at the youngest age possible. Childhood is the time of the greatest learning availability. Young minds are like clean slates, with the most space to write on. Young minds are also like sponges, which are capable of absorbing things beyond what is readily evident.

Overindulgence of children can foster dependence. Learning that things are coming to you as an entitlement, without expending some sort of effort in return, can prove detrimental. Good behavior may be rewarded but bad behavior should likewise merit appropriate correction. It is important to give children chores to do and some form of regimentation so that they are properly prepared for school with the sense of discipline and respect that is expected at home. Disrespect at home often translates to disrespect for teachers and in the broader sense to defiance against authorities.

Studies have shown that discipline of this kind is often waived in divorced families, as parents compete for children's affections with unsolicited gifts and favors. Proper disciplinary actions are best applied when there appears to be a unified approach from both parents. Whenever possible, even divorced parents should act as a team when it comes to the imparting of required disciplinary action for the child's benefit. Do not interfere with the progress in a child's development by projecting your own guilty feelings at not having been the best parent for whatever reason. Do not make the child a victim of parental competition or marital discord.

Children, at the youngest age they can be perceived to understand, should be taught to respect not only authority but also money—what it can buy and what it can give them. Teach that money can buy them items, but it also can buy them freedom and the time to be free enough to do the things that brings them their greatest pleasure.

The history of freedom being bought with money is interesting and important. It goes back about twenty-five hundred years to the ancient Greeks. In antiquity, all commerce was conducted through barter. You would trade me your cow for a number of my chickens or a horse for a plow. Although coins had been manufactured in China since half a millennium earlier, the minting of precious metal coins was not widespread until the classical period of Greek culture. Since wealth in antiquity was measured by possessions on the ground, value could not be easily transported and most people could not travel far from home. With the availability of coins of value, people became free to travel, since they now had exchangeable money they could easily take with them wherever they went. Money was able to buy freedom for people to do what they wanted to do.

Children should be taught to be good and generous people, with love and compassion, but also with a sense of responsibility. The more effective this teaching is at the beginning of the learning process, the better the outcome in adulthood.

Childhood education in this regard should begin with menial task assignments, like helping to set the dining room table for dinner, taking out the trash, shoveling snow and other duties, with suitable rewards for this labor. No matter how small the payment, this teaches the child that work brings rewards. Refusal to do the work requested should earn admonishment.

No matter how rich you are, teaching children respect for labor and money is important for character development in all societies. While this type of upbringing will not give you a guarantee that your children will all be successfully employed, it does give you the best hope that they will grow up with the motivation to be self-sufficient and not have to rely on their retired or near-retired parents to support them.

Always encourage childhood entrepreneurship. Helping them set up a curbside lemonade stand may lead to exploring ideas in the family garage. Some of the greatest industrial and technological innovations have begun with adolescent tinkering. Supporting your children in this way ultimately may prove beneficial for us all.[14]

7. The affluent typically invest wisely.

They know that serendipitous opportunities occur infrequently, so they respond aggressively when such occasions arise. They heed the wise words of investment greats like Warren Buffett and his mentor Benjamin Graham, who counsel to be brave when others are fearful and to be fearful when others are exuberant. They know that nothing goes up or down forever. They know when to buy and at what price they want to sell at the time that they buy. Since you can never go broke selling at a profit, when they reach that price they sell. Knowing full well that no one knows where the bottom price is, very few buy at the very bottom or sell at the very top. Financial success is obtained by continually realizing profits somewhere in the middle. When they buy into the well-researched stock of a growing company with a good management team, they remain for the duration, knowing that some ventures are for the long term and are not deterred by day-to-day price fluctuations.

8. The affluent make wise decisions.

They choose the right occupations. Sometimes choosing the wrong way to make a living can be detrimental. If you have to keep switching careers, seniority, with whatever privileges it brings, will be lost. Switching careers can be costly if there is a long time of unemployment between jobs or if expensive retraining is required. Making the correct choice of a life's work is important, not only for financial reasons, but for personal fulfilment as well.[15]

On many occasions I have given thanks for having chosen what turned out to be the perfect vocation for me. When I was in my psychiatric residency, I earned my room and board in the quarters of a general hospital by lecturing to the interns and residents of other medical specialties and making psychiatric clinical presentations. At that time I befriended a surgical resident. I helped introduce him to a girl I had once dated, who subsequently became his wife. After graduating from our respective training programs we went our separate ways. Practicing in two different states, we rarely met. I was surprised some fifteen years later to receive a telephone call from him, requesting that I see him and his wife. He was conflicted about his surgical practice and wanted my advice about seeking training in psychiatry. His wife, a strikingly pretty girl when I knew her, was still attractive but now showed the dismay and concern of a more mature woman. Psychiatry and surgery are about as distant as two medical specialties can be and usually attract doctors of different personality types.

Basically the surgeon deals with a patient as a person who has a complaint about his or her body. It is a person-to-body relationship. Surgery is involved with anatomy, with physically handling and altering body parts. While the surgeon may listen intently to the patient's complaints, there rarely becomes an intimate person-to-person relationship, unless they have social contact as well. Only in special cases does the surgeon become involved with the life of the patient outside of the pathology of the disease. In many cases it is of benefit for the patient that the surgeon is distant and not emotionally involved. Surgery is very strenuous and a physically (as well as emotionally) demanding specialty. Having a patient's life at stake on a daily basis and often witnessing death can provoke anxiety and many have to maintain a professional detachment to keep from paying a grave personal price. Surgery demands manual dexterity and extreme concentration and this may be more difficult if there is an emotional attachment to the patient. For their own protection and because of their personality makeup, many surgeons maintain an aloofness and an emotional distance from their patients. Therefore, many surgeons have been accused of having a poor bedside manner and little apparent care for their patients. Recognizing this, some medical training centers have introduced courses in proper doctor-patient relationships into their training programs.

Psychiatry, on the other hand, is a medical specialty which demands an intimate delving into the core of the patient's psyche. Psychotherapy explores and promotes the sharing of the most intimate details of the patient's life. The most intensive of the depth therapies, psychoanalysis, even uses the relationship of the patient to the therapist and the therapist to the patient as a therapeutic tool. Opposite to the surgeon who has to emotionally distance himself from involvement, the psychiatrist, in order to be effective, has to project a caring yet objective and non-judgmental persona. The psychiatrist wants to share his patient's life experiences. Much of psychotherapy has do with the support and creation of a benevolent environment to allow trust, so that emotional expression can be freely shared.

These two very different medical specialties attract candidates with different personalities and character traits. My friend who came to me for guidance fell somewhere in the middle. He was not steeled enough to escape the emotional demands of a surgical practice but he was not nearly capable of projecting the empathetic involvement required for tolerating a daily one-on-one battle against mental illness. What he required was a rest period and a better understanding of himself. Trying to be something he could not be would have substituted eventual misery for the anxiety which he had begun to feel in the operating room. After a fruitful therapeutic session and a long-needed vacation, he returned to his surgical practice refreshed and was very successful. We must be who we are and we should only do what we can do.

Having to give up the work we love prematurely because of outside factors can be cause for anger and frustration, but having to do so because of our own miscalculations can cause severe depression, because, at its core, depression is anger turned inward. One naval commander, having served with distinction as a first officer on a ship, was in line to be promoted to captain with his own command. Just before his promotion came through, his wife was diagnosed with cancer.

He had great pride in himself and demanded the respect of his subordinates. His finest pleasure was viewing the sunset from the deck of a ship at sea. Despite this love for his work, he felt his first duty was to his wife and he resigned from the navy to care for her. Expecting her to cope with the disease for years, he anticipated being a caregiver for a long time. Unfortunately, her cancer spread quickly and after only two months she died. He was left to grieve not only for his wife, but also to be self-recriminating over the unwise choice he had made. He became reclusive, speaking only to his daughter who became alarmed at his condition. Over and over again he chastised himself for not waiting, not delaying his resignation. He tortured himself into a deep depression. After a prolonged period of mourning and self-examination he had the realization that he had no good choice to make and that he couldn't have abandoned his dying wife and gone to sea in good conscience. He had done his best to care for the person he loved and he learned to be grateful for the time they had together at the end of her life due to his decision.

If you are among those who love what they do and can't wait to get to work each day, give thanks for your blessing. Having experienced that kind of love relationship with my practice, I know that the feeling goes far beyond how much money you make or how much respect you get. The sages have taught us that to save a life is like saving the whole world. I have been blessed to have participated in the saving of several lives. There are few times during the course of a lifetime when we can feel like heroes. Getting a hit to win a baseball game, scoring a winning touchdown—these pale in comparison to saving a life.

One day, over forty years ago, while I was at my desk taking a break between seeing patients in my office, I received an emergency phone call from a suicidal patient. She told me, in a faint voice, that she had swallowed a lot of tranquilizer pills and was just calling me to say goodbye. It was a very sad case. This unmarried woman had been diagnosed with vaginal cancer at age thirty-two. The surgery and follow-up treatment had left her unable to engage in any sexual activity. She lapsed into a deep post-operative depression requiring several psychiatric hospitalizations and out-patient psychotherapy, including medicating with antidepressants and antipsychotic drugs. At one point her depression got so severe that she required a series of electroconvulsive (shock) treatments. We formed a strong bond in therapy and I knew her call was a cry for help. She lived in a first floor apartment just around the corner from my office and I calculated that I could get to her quicker than an ambulance would if I dialed 911, so I headed out to the parking lot, grabbed my car and parked it illegally right in front of her house. Luckily she was a small woman weighing barely ninety pounds and the door to her apartment was not locked. I picked her up, slapping her face to keep her awake, and threw her over my shoulder. I carried her down to my car and laid her down in the front passenger seat.

I kept talking to her and slapping her face until we reached the emergency room entrance where hospital personnel—I had called from her apartment after ascertaining she was still alive—were waiting with a gurney to take her in to pump her stomach.

The procedure was successful. Her vital signs returned to normal. However, she could no longer live alone. Having served in the WAC (Women's Army Corps), she was eligible for long-term government care and was transferred to a retirement home, where she lived until she died a natural death.

That episode left me believing that if I wasn't destined to accomplish another useful thing in my life, I had already served my purpose. I had saved a life. There are probably firefighters, policemen and surgeons who get the opportunity much more often, but the feeling that comes with that accomplishment made all the years of study, training and hardship worthwhile.

Doing what you love doesn't guarantee financial success, but it sure makes the quest more gratifying. Learning who you are and what gratifies you is vital in choosing the right occupation on the road to success. Just like knowing what to order from the dinner menu at a restaurant, you have to listen to your instincts and choose wisely.

9. Affluent people are knowledgeable about taxes.

If you add together income tax, both state and federal, state and city sales tax, real estate tax, capital gains tax, Social Security and Medicare costs, the average American family pays their governments about one-half of their income; in some countries, citizens pay more. That means Americans work from January until June supporting the government and only from July through December do we earn for ourselves. While it is every citizen's duty to file a tax return and pay what is due, it is every citizen's right to use legal manipulation and loopholes to avoid overpaying. Most of the general public do not know enough about what they are entitled to deduct under our voluminous tax code. This goes for rich people too. Many rich people hire accounting experts who do know how to save them money. Undoubtedly, there are people who would get more in return than the cost of the accountant and it would save the hassle of doing something you were not trained to do.

To aid a professional in getting you as much back from the government as you are legally entitled to, you should start a carefully-labeled filing system showing every category of your expenditures. These should include every detail of your work, medical care, travel and job-related clothing expenses and any other expenditure which could conceivably warrant deductions, like for children, education and the like. It is your job to get that file to the tax expert in as usable a fashion as possible. Start the file the first day of each year and put in every applicable receipt in as categorized a fashion as possible. Every form from banks and brokerage houses which indicates that duplicates are being made available to the Internal Revenue Service (IRS) must be included. Remember, the less cluttered and the better organized the file, the less time your accountant will need to sort things out and the more time he or she will have to work on saving you money. Throwing all your receipts into a box at the last minute and then dumping the box on the accountant's desk is not wise.

Saving money from your tax bill can add up over the years. For example, if you keep $2000 a year away from the tax man and let it compound at 5 percent interest, after forty years you would have accrued in the neighborhood of $100,000. Using tax-advantaged investing is important in building wealth.[16]

10. The last of the ten steps of becoming like the affluent is acquiring knowledge and insight about what is going on in the world and applying that to the betterment of one's self.

For example, learn what a rising world power did to aid its economy and apply it to an individual family's planning for retirement.[17]

China has grown economically from the pack of emerging market nations to become the second largest economy in the world. A lot of this has to do, I believe, with their instituting population control. Chinese leaders realized that if they allowed their population, which had exceeded one billion people, to grow unabated, they would not be able to improve per capita income and would remain a poor nation. They studied the world's economies and saw that African countries like Mali, with some of the world's highest birth rates, were also among the poorest and countries like Singapore, with one of the lowest birth rates, were among the richest. They instituted the one-child-per-family rule (since relaxed, allowing two children if one parent is an only child, due to the worrisome aging of the population). Even with the relaxation of the rule, many Chinese families still choose to have one child. The Chinese have learned that with a population now over 1.3 billion and over 400 million still living in poverty, the road to economic stability could be paved by curtailing population growth.

In contrast to the successful Chinese experiment, which has elevated China to being a world power, the African nations, with unabated bloated birthrates, are wallowing in poverty, disease and, in numerous cases, political instability. The African continent is rife with insurrection and regional wars. The poor are so desperate that some have stooped to committing unspeakable horrors on their fellow Africans. To raise money, the criminals have come to demand ransoms from kidnappings and piracy. The world's worst poverty has elicited charity and benevolent aid from many sources. The victims of atrocities, rapes and other evil acts have come to represent the worst that mankind has to offer in its twenty-first century brutality. In the midst of the AIDS and Ebola epidemics, deaths from malaria and attempted genocides, children are being poured into this cauldron of poverty and disease.

Whereas the Chinese have learned to advance economically, many of the African nations remain beholden to their neighbors and the world at large.

Strictly from a retirement-centered point of view, learning from the actions of world planners and being able to integrate this into your own lifestyle is helpful in achieving the affluence you seek. The successful end result, being able to close the deal in a favorable manner as the affluent have learned to do, is the goal to strive toward.

POST-WORK

In the previous parts of this book, we have dealt with the requirements of psychological, practical and financial planning for a successful retirement. In the next part we will explore in detail the choices to be made during the last few years leading up to and after retirement. We have been concerned with the accumulation of wealth; now we shall be concerned with the handling and allocation of that wealth. We will discuss the most effective ways to allow the money we've made to support and sustain us and how we should react to this, how we should alter our situations if necessary and how we may maintain the contentment and security we deserve.

CHAPTER 8

Funding for Retirement

I feel strongly that, whenever possible, the best way to reduce the difficulty of the transitional period from working to being unemployed is by doing it gradually. When I decided to retire, I had a choice to make. Since I had a thriving practice which had value, I could have taken in a younger associate, indoctrinated him into the practice and worked out a buyout plan, or I could have just stopped taking on new patients and gradually reduced the size of the practice, working less and less until I was ready to quit and then turn over my caseload to a colleague.

Since the figures, counting my new associate's salary, would come out about the same, I opted to do the latter. I went from working five days a week to four, taking off Fridays to enjoy longer weekends. Eventually I took off Mondays as well, to enjoy even longer weekends. I stopped all institutional work. I referred any patients requiring hospitalization to other physicians. When I had reduced the number of patients I was seeing so that I only needed to come to the office two days a week, I began to prepare my remaining patients for their being transferred to the care of another psychiatrist and started the necessary paperwork and psychotherapy for the transferral. As many of the last patients to leave my care had been with me for a long time, it was necessary for me to engage in intensive end-stage therapy to lessen separation anxiety.

I realize that not all jobs or professions may afford you the luxury of being able to exit work gradually the way I did. Nor may you want to do it this way. It does take knowing yourself and your situation to determine if you want to leave abruptly or gradually. For me it worked out perfectly, without hassle or complaint. I gave notice to the owner of the center city building that housed my office and when my lease was up, with some great memories still fresh in my mind as I looked around my empty office, I closed my door for the last time.

It was not easy, after more than one-half century, no longer getting up early in the morning and preparing to go to work. No longer being intimately involved in the lives of people who entrusted their emotional well-being to my care. No longer doing what I had trained for. What I had worked and studied for. The sleepless nights, the exams, the years of sacrifice that became the past. I felt uncertainty at what lay ahead. Was I really ready for this? Did I plan this out well enough? What would I do to fill my time?

ENDGAME

Nearing retirement, your thinking needs to be refocused. What was once of primary importance no longer may be. Worries and insecurities of yesteryear may have dissipated or even been eliminated. Long-term thinking may have been replaced with a shorter outlook on specific items or things in general. What was once a luxury may now be a necessity and what was once a necessity may now have become a luxury. Time changes all things; when there is time to recollect and reflect, some concerns seem to vanish. In the endgame there is no longer the need or emotionality to go with mundane life occurrences. A lot has already been spent on both the trifling and the important and the years need to mellow the responses. This is no longer a time for anxiety. Our bodies do not handle that as well as before. It is no longer a time for over-evaluation. It is a time to put everything into a benevolent, calm, mature perspective.

PARTIAL RETIREMENT

My gradual retirement took about five years. Somewhere during the third year, when I was working three days a week, I felt very contented. My wife and I were able to enjoy getting away for long weekends and we felt at ease taking two and three-week vacations instead of the seven-to-ten-day holidays to which we were accustomed. I was still making enough money to accommodate our life-style and the added time together was enjoyable. Although I had burned some professional bridges, like giving up my institutional work, I could still go on as things were without totally closing my office. At this point I gave the concept of a partial retirement important consideration.

In my years of doing forensic psychiatric work and testifying as an expert witness on occasion, I had come across a number of attorneys who had the designation "of counsel." They maintained a relationship with the law firm at which they had their office space, but were no longer associates or partners of that firm. Some of the older lawyers worked part of the time. So I was well acquainted with the idea of being a part-time professional.

After a period of self-evaluation and reassessing my goals, I chose to continue on to full retirement. Yet it was tempting to remain in part-time practice for a longer or even indefinite period. My wife's prodding helped me make my final decision. After a long career in social work, she was sure she wanted to be fully retired and had no hesitation in making her desires known. The more I thought about it, the more I believed it was the right decision for her and I.

Partial retirement still remains a good option for those uncertain about fully leaving their work.

FINANCIAL PSYCHOLOGY

In an interview, the Secretary of Labor said that the average age of skilled workers such as electricians, pipefitters and the like in the United States is currently fifty-nine and a half years.[18] The workforce is aging. They soon will be retiring. We desperately need a widespread system of apprenticeships to fill the upcoming deficit of skilled laborers. Companies can't find enough skilled workers to satisfy their needs.

As more and more of these workers across the nation retire, most having accumulated a significant amount of money in their retirement accounts, the total amounts have grown to a staggering figure. An estimated one-third of all American money resides in retirement accounts.

The penchant for self-management is understandable, since 80 percent of professional money managers, those who run mutual funds and hedge funds, fail to produce results as profitable as investing in the stock market as a whole. Another reason for the large number of self-determined retirement accounts is the recent volatility of the stock market. Many saw their retirement funds cut in half during the second-greatest market collapse within eighty years. Not since the Great Depression of the early decades of the twentieth century did such a large percentage of investors panic and sell their holdings at a sizeable loss. Since then, despite the recovery of the stock markets, many have retained their fear of investing in stocks.

Another factor is that of trust. The credibility of the investing community as a whole has been assaulted. We constantly get media reports of insider trading, even involving government officials. We hear of unsuspecting victims of Ponzi schemes losing their life savings.

Reporters repeatedly break stories of illegal activity at our largest banks. Many companies are paying huge fines for stock manipulations detrimental to their investors. With my modest portfolio, I am involved in at least a dozen class action lawsuits, against some of the largest and best-known companies I have invested in over the years, for activities that I wouldn't even have known about if I weren't notified of my participation in the lawsuits.

This crisis of trust has driven many people away from active investing, to seek safer havens for their money. Historically the alternative to stocks has been bonds, but during this period of recovery from our recent recession interest rates have been kept very low, so that the interest payouts from bonds would be insufficient to fund the retirement requirements of many retirees.

PASSIVE INCOME

There are financial products available for those of large and small means which remove retirees from having to oversee their own affairs and pay out specified amounts of money on a regular basis. It must be stated that these retirement vehicles are the products of profit-making companies. They are as safe as the company you are dealing with, so it is imperative that you purchase one of these from a well-known company that has been in business for a long time, has survived many financial crises and is highly rated by the rating agencies. Since these companies are selling you something, you must realize that their profit and their salesperson's commission is somehow being taken out of your funds. Therefore, from an income point of view, these are not considered to be the most advantageous retirement investments.

ANNUITIES

If the retiree has adequate funds to finance a comfortable retirement but docs not have the time or inclination to monitor the stock market, he or she might consider annuities.

An annuity is a contract between an individual and the insurance company issuing the annuity. It promises a minimum income with a claim that this value will not decrease with market downturns and may even grow in times of appreciating markets, depending on the performance of the managed securities backing the guarantee.

The most noticeable initial drawback to an annuity is the contract itself. They are usually lengthy and complex and obviously have been drawn up by a bevy of legal experts to the advantage of the issuers. They are often so complicated that many of the insurance agents who are trying to talk you into this agreement so they can earn a commission do not fully understand all the details. The contract must be reviewed carefully, to become aware of every detail. Since there are different types of annuities, it is important not to choose the wrong one or you may get stuck in a long-term contract that will not allow you to reach your retirement goals.

Annuities differ in how premium payments are made, in the timing of payouts and in the investment options they offer.

Close to retirement, when there is a large amount of money available, a single premium plan, I feel, would appear to be most appropriate. The single lump of cash is invested into an income-producing annuity, where regular payments begin to be received within the first year. These single premium, immediate payment annuities can be set up to make payments for a defined number of years or for life. This gives the retiree a continuous flow of income, with the management of assets taken care of within the framework of the contract.

If the annuity option is exercised earlier in life, perhaps many years prior to retirement, then it can be set up to be funded like other retirement accounts by making monthly or annual contributions over a period of time. Since immediate income would not yet be required with this flexible premium payment plan, it can be bundled with a deferred annuity, wherein income payments are deferred for some period allowing the value to grow. This can be done with whichever investment option is chosen. After retirement or upon contract maturity, the contract value can be taken as a lump sum or, through a process called annuitization, converted to an immediate income annuity.

Annuity investment options include both fixed and variable plans. Investing in a fixed annuity is like buying a Certificate of Deposit (CD) from a bank or a brokerage company. It promises no loss of principal and guarantees a certain rate of interest. However, the interest rates are not permanent and can change after a pre-determined period, which may be as short as one year. Depending on market conditions, interest rates may be lower than other investments.

Variable annuities are the most popular annuities for those who are making periodic premium payments. Typically, they invest in groups of mutual funds under an insurance package and are available through investment firms in conjunction with insurers. They have the highest potential for growth of the annuity plans, but also the potential for the greatest volatility. They also usually incur the highest annual fees, as much as 4 percent, which cut substantially into earnings. Earnings are not taxed until they are withdrawn, but once they are withdrawn they are taxed as regular income, not capital gains. Some variable annuities offer the ability to buy riders with enhanced benefits like guaranteed minimum withdrawal options. While contract owners have the right to participate in the choice of funds in which to be invested, insurers may place restrictions on the percent to be placed in fixed-income allocations, like bonds and cash, as opposed to stocks. Although variable annuities have been the most popular annuities sold, as they offer mutual fund investment options with insurance-related guarantees, because of the investment restrictions and the fees the earnings are historically quite less than if the money were invested in an S&P 500 index fund.

Equity-indexed annuities are fixed annuities that offer minimum and maximum interest rates based on stock market index returns. There are no stocks or bonds held in the annuity; the returns are simply based on the market index performance. They have recently become popular mainly because the principal is not subject to volatility, while retaining the ability to grow in value. However, factors like participation rates and performance caps can limit growth. Historically these annuities have returned a higher yield than high-rated bonds, but have underperformed the stock indexes themselves.

In this age of great fear of outliving your money and market uncertainty, investors may be drawn to annuities because of their so-called guarantees. Once again the guarantee is only as good as the company issuing the annuity. So I would advise only dealing with well-established insurance companies. If you have any doubts about an insurer, you can consult the online services of the A.M. Best Company of Oldwick, New Jersey. The Best Company is a Nationally Recognized Statistical Rating Organization (NRSRO), as designated by the United States Securities and Exchange Commission, which specializes in rating the financial strength of insurance companies.

The guarantees of insurance companies come with negatives. These include special fees, withdrawal limits and also strict requirements investors must adhere to in order to merit the guarantees. Many of the guarantees are features of additional benefit riders which come with added costs.

You should always be aware when entrusting your money to a profit-making company to invest for you that they will take not only what they earn from your money above what they pay you back, but will also tack on fees for any additional benefits bought. Among the additional benefit riders that can be purchased are enhanced death benefits, guaranteed income for life, guaranteed growth factors and long-term-care insurance. By far the most chosen of these is the guaranteed lifetime withdrawal benefit. This rider guarantees that the withdrawal of a specified percentage of the contract value can be made every year for the lifetime of the annuity purchaser. Other riders guarantee minimum income benefits, minimum accumulation benefits and minimum withdrawal benefits which, if the contract gains value over time, are totally unnecessary.

Just about all annuities act like life insurance policies in case of the death of the annuity holder. The basic death benefit returns the initial premium amount, minus any withdrawals or the current cash value, whichever is larger, to the heirs. This guaranteed return of principal, upon death, is an advantage that annuities have over non-insurance-backed investments.

In addition to the basic death benefit, which returns the initial premium, there are enhanced death benefit options available for additional fees that pay out amounts greater than the original premium.

Since annuity value gains are treated as a taxable gain to your beneficiaries, the insurance companies have devised tax coverage enhanced benefits which pay out additional sums to cover the taxes. This would, however, be of no benefit in cases where there were no gains realized.

770 ACCOUNTS

Since there is so much money being allocated for retirement, the insurance industry in the United States is attempting to market various products to augment traditional retirement plans. One of these is covered by the Internal Revenue Service (IRS) regulation 7702. These have come to be known as 770 accounts or 7702 plans. These products are not retirement plans. They are life insurance policies with life as well as death benefits, which can be structured to pay out tax-free benefits.

There are various restrictions and regulations required for these policies to function as beneficial retirement vehicles. The policy has to be issued by a mutual insurance company and be a participating whole life policy. It has to have appropriate riders to facilitate minimizing death benefits and thereby maximizing benefits during the lifetime of the policy holder, tax-free distributions, tax-deferred growth and even disability benefits until age sixty-five.

The advantage that these policies have over other retirement plans is that there is no limitation on how much life insurance you can buy. This feature would appeal to those retirees with considerable money to invest. Also, the cash value is protected against creditors and death benefits are passed on to beneficiaries tax free.

By minimizing death benefits, the cash value and living benefits are maximized. This differs from traditional life insurance policies with maximized death benefits, where there is no cash value accumulated for three to five years to accommodate the insurance agent's fee. While your cash value account increases each year, in a life insurance policy it may be many years before you will be able to get back what you put in.

Most money managers feel that only people who have contributed the maximum to their 401(k) plan and have additional money available for retirement funding should consider purchasing whole life insurance. Some policies have as much as 9 percent embedded commissions for the insurance salesperson over the life of the policy. This is far more than other investment fees.

The great problem around the world with an aging population is what is going to happen to those individuals who have insufficient money put away to fund an adequate retirement. The traditional American dream is to own one's home and many families have a majority of their savings tied up in their houses. Realizing this dilemma, the US government sponsored a plan that allows mortgage lenders to issue Home Equity Conversion Mortgages. This allows seniors sixty-two years and older with sufficient equity in their homes to receive funds to help with their living expenses.

REVERSE MORTGAGES

A home equity conversion or *reverse mortgage* is basically a nonrecourse loan based on the appraised value of the property owned. It is encumbered as a lien against the property. It is treated as a tax-free loan with your home as collateral.

You may choose to receive the payments in a single large amount, monthly, as a line of credit or as a combination of these options. You are free to remain in your home, no longer required to make any mortgage payments. All payments made to you are tax-free. If you die while still residing in your home, your heirs will not be personally liable if the balance on your loan exceeds the value of the home. If your heirs choose to pay off the reverse mortgage and there is remaining equity, they will inherit the remaining equity.

One should always be aware that these reverse mortgages are products of profit-making mortgage lenders and there are sizeable fees and expenses involved. Home equity conversion mortgage loan balances increase over time. As the proceeds are spent, the value of the estate inheritance may decrease over time. Fees should be expected to be higher than with a traditional mortgage. There are initial and annual Federal Housing Administration (FHA) insurance premiums to be paid. Loan origination fees should also be expected to be higher than with traditional mortgages.

While it may seem extreme to advise people to place their home equity up for collateral, preventing their heirs, in most cases, from inheriting the family home, the reverse mortgage is a viable option for those who really have few other choices. It is recommended only for those individuals who have a great majority of their wealth tied up in their home property and insufficient income from other investments to fund retirement. The retirees can remain in their home as long as the last surviving partner remains there, with a grace period of a specified time for any required nursing home or similar stay of absence.

Since reverse mortgage advertisements are now widespread and would probably attract only those poorer seniors who are strapped for cash for other things besides retirement, like home repairs, it is important for them to understand that although Social Security and Medicare eligibility are not affected by a reverse mortgage loan, needs-based government programs like Medicaid may be impacted.

The proceeds obtained from a home equity conversion mortgage can be used for anything on which the borrower wants to spend the money. This availability of ready cash for people in need has seen the number of reverse mortgages administered by Housing and Urban Development (HUD) increase dramatically in the last decade. The amount that can be borrowed depends upon the age of the borrower, the value of the home, current interest rates and the amount of the loan fees. Home equity conversion mortgage loans are federally insured.

From a pure investment point of view, the reverse mortgage is not as great an investment vehicle for the borrower as it is for the lender. The loans are front-loaded, which means sizeable up-front costs are taken out of the home equity value at the closing of the deal, making it very profitable for the mortgage company from the start. As with conventional mortgages, reverse mortgage lenders make money through interest, origination fees and points. The interest rate varies according to the market. Because reverse mortgages still make up a very small portion of the total mortgage market and reverse mortgage buyers are more limited in options, closing costs are significantly higher than with traditional mortgages.

Reverse mortgage borrowers must understand that they are still required to pay real estate taxes, carry homeowners insurance and be responsible for home repairs. They also have to pay for mortgage insurance to guarantee that the lender will receive full repayment. This protects the lender from loss in case of a decrease in the property's value. Mortgage insurance also protects the lender if the borrowers live to a very old age with the mortgage thus being held for a long time, which allows the accrued interest on the loan to exceed the value of the property.

When a home property appreciates in value, the reverse mortgage acts like a conventional mortgage. The lender only gets back what is owed. After the price of the loan, all fees and interest are repaid, the balance goes to the homeowner or heirs.

In America, federal legislation allows a $500,000 exemption for home value to be counted as an asset when considering Medicaid eligibility, as long as the home remains occupied and no payments are received from the home's equity. Depending on which state the homeowner resides in, the proceeds of a reverse mortgage may block eligibility for Medicaid, which considers such proceeds as assets.

People residing in socialistically-oriented societies can look forward to government-controlled pensions upon retiring, which may or may not lift them above the poverty level. In parts of Europe and Asia, family care for the aged is more the norm than in the United States, where families may be more mobile and children may live far away from their parents and grandparents.

Few investment considerations carry the emotional impact of deciding to relinquish your home upon leaving it without passing it on to your heirs. This may mean that old, poor people have to give up the dream of an adult lifetime: leaving their major asset to their children. This, coupled with locating the most reputable lender in their area, can be a difficult decision. Lobbying from their heirs can complicate matters even more.

Great care should always be taken in choosing a lender and adequate research is advised. There might be HUD-approved counselors in the area who are totally independent of any transaction and can be of assistance. For people who have little, the lure of receiving a large amount of money is a temptation to make unwise decisions and therefore experienced advisers should be sought out. Above all else, the specifications as to the length of absence from the home before loss of residence is incurred must be understood. The greatest tragedy would be to lose the house and become homeless. So if an older invalid has to leave the home for a period of nursing home care, it must be fully understood when they have to return in order to maintain ownership.

Reverse mortgages are not recommended for people who require a large sum of money, for whatever reason, and are capable of making payments on a home equity loan. A reverse mortgage is the answer of last resort for funding the retirement of people whose only major source of equity is their home property and who have no other source of income except perhaps insufficient Social Security benefits.

DIVIDENDS

Benjamin Graham, an American professional investor, is considered to be the initial proponent of value investing. He was the mentor of the most successful of all value investors, Warren Buffet, at Columbia University Business School. Graham has said: "Basically, price fluctuations have only one significant meaning for the true investor. They provide him an opportunity to buy wisely when prices fall sharply and to sell wisely when they advance a great deal. At other times he will do better if he forgets about the stock market and pays attention to his dividend returns and to the operating results of his companies."[19]

Along with other income-producing investments, dividend-paying common stocks should be the lifeblood of any self-directed retirement portfolio. Not only do dividend stocks have less volatility year after year than non-dividend-paying stocks, they statistically outperform them as well. Dividend-producing stocks typically have lower risk and offer higher returns over the long run.

A recent research study found that from 1972 through 2013, non-dividend-paying stocks earned only 2.3 percent per year; dividend-paying stocks provided a 9.3 percent annual return. Those stocks which not only paid a dividend, but raised it year after year, generated a compound annual return of 10.1 percent.[20]

According to this study, the difference in compound growth is astounding. A $100,000 investment in non-dividend-paying stocks in 1972 would have grown to about $250,000 in 2013, while a $100,000 investment in dividend-paying stocks would have grown to about $3,750,000 and the same amount invested in dividend-growing stocks would have appreciated to over $5,000,000.[21]

Investors often forget that stocks are really ownership certificates in companies and that people go into business not only to appreciate their capital assets but to draw payments, like wages. During up markets investors tend to forget this, go only for glamorous growth stocks and forget about depending on dividend income they may not yet need for day-to-day expenditures. Successful investment for and during retirement depends not only on maximizing growth during up markets, but also minimizing depreciation in down markets. After retirement it is also necessary to generate income and there is nothing better than having a bevy of low-risk, dividend-paying stocks to go along with a basket of interest-paying fixed-income investments, in a balanced income-producing portfolio with potential for growth.

The final investment objective in preparation for retirement is the creation of a group of investments which are capable of producing sufficient income to fund your desired lifestyle while still growing your net worth, so that you can meet unexpected emergencies and keep up with inflation.

CHAPTER 9

Living Arrangements

One of the most important preparations for retirement is the decision on what to change about where and how the retirees will live. Should they stay where they are, perhaps near children and grandchildren, or move to a different climate zone? What is most important to satisfy needs for enjoyment? Are they skiers and should they move to a snowy mountain community? Or do they love the sea, opting instead for a southern shore area? If they are boaters they will want to be near water. Will it be a lake, a river or the ocean? If they are golfers they may want to be in a locale offering affordable golf club memberships and a climate conducive to year-round playing conditions. Fishermen may want to be near bodies of water that accommodate their sport. Deep-sea sport fishermen would want to be near the ocean, where they might have room to troll, while those satisfied with smaller game may choose a stocked lake. Fly fishermen would want a stream nearby their new home.

For those who can afford it, to be able to satisfy many desires, two or more homes may be required. The decision of how many retirement residences to have is a major one if money is in doubt, but if there are adequate funds to support two or more homes, keeping multiple abodes may be the solution. This would allow closeness to family at least part of the year, while allowing escape from the harshness of unpleasant weather the rest of the year. Also, having living arrangements in two climates might allow participation in various recreational activities that are not available in one area alone. It might allow year-round participation in a favorite activity.

Having two residences need not only be an option for the very wealthy. In America, many middle-income families with modest homes in the North venture south to live in trailer parks during the winter months. Others who don't want the expense of owning two homes rent homes or condominiums for weeks or months to enjoy the beach in the North during the summer or in the South to escape the winter cold. Owning one home and renting another saves the expense of having to pay additional taxes, insurance costs and worrying about storm and other house damage.

Historically, Americans have been a mobile people. During working years, when a better job opportunity opens up in another town, state or country, if it represents a good advancement we accept the challenge. Often this means uprooting the family and taking kids away from their schools and friends, requiring a period of adjustment. Retirement is also an adjustment period. It may mean distancing yourself from familiar things, family and friends. Retirement may require a rebalancing of your sense of values.

Preparation for retirement, if you have unprecedented freedom, may mean a choice between desirable options. Things and even people previously held most dear may have to find a position of lesser importance in the scheme of your new life. Old friends, although still held dear but from afar, may be replaced by new ones who are now near. To each retiree, occasions have different value and significance. A distant relative dies, whose funeral you would never miss when you lived in the same city, but now that it's many miles away via an expensive plane flight which might aggravate your arthritic pain, you phone or write your condolences instead. These are the types of attitude adjustments which are necessitated by the effects of the geographical change and the aging process itself.

A *Wall Street Journal* article noted that due to the influx of wealth from the stock market and real estate, retirees who had tended to stay close to their original homes have begun to migrate in great numbers to southern and western states. The article noted that states like Florida and Arizona, which have tax laws and climates that attract seniors, have been among the greatest recipients of these relocated retirees. Besides lower taxes in southern states and a haven from brutal winter weather, retirees, especially from the northeastern part of the country, want to take advantage of the cheaper home prices in the South. According to a survey of the National Association of Realtors, homes cost about 33 percent less in the South than in the northeastern part of the United States.[22]

As older people tend to have more weather-related pain syndromes than younger people, it is compelling for seniors to consider relocating to states with warmer climates. This is reflected in the relative population growth of various American cities. Among the ten fastest growing cities in 2013, those in Arizona, Texas and North Carolina were among the leaders: Raleigh, North Carolina; Phoenix, Arizona; and Austin, Dallas, San Antonio and Houston, all in the state of Texas.[23]

The decision of what to do with the rest of your life, which with good dietary habits and modern medicine can last for many years, in an atmosphere of increased freedom of choice, is a very important one and should be thought out carefully. You should consider all the elements involved. Focus on what would be most fulfilling in the last years of your life. All psychological, practical and financial aspects should be contemplated.

More and more retirees are choosing to live in retirement communities or retirement villages. The social advantages of living in close proximity to people of your own age, with easily accessible recreational and medical facilities, is quite a compelling argument for this style of life. Gregarious individuals, who have previously enjoyed the country club atmosphere with many close friends and the parties and social events that ensued from such relationships and who would miss this in solitary relocation, would readily acclimate to recapture that lifestyle.

Seniors are more active now than they were in generations past. The advancement of the sciences has made us aware of the importance of exercise and keeping fit in warding off cardio-vascular disease. Special regimens have been developed to allow seniors to participate in activities not recommended in times past. Geriatric practice has become an accepted medical specialty, which exclusively studies the diseases of older adults. Gerontologists— not only those in the domain of medicine—are doing research in the fields of biology, optometry, dentistry, physical and occupa-tional therapy, social work, recreation therapy, psychology, psychi-atry, economics, political science, architecture, geography, urban planning, pharmacy, public health, anthropology and housing with regard to the aging process.

People age differently, in stages, in relation to chronological age. Biological factors are also involved, related to the effective-ness of organ function. Also in play are the psychological func-tioning of sensory and perceptual processes, cognitive abilities, adaptive capacity and personality traits. The eroding of social skills is important in adaptation to changing roles with regard to family and friends and other societal relationships. These vari-ous parameters together measure the true functional age of the individual, allowing some people to excel at activities long beyond their peer average. A lot has to do with genetics, but exercise regi-mens and continued mental stimulation are important to keep the biological and psychological equipment honed.

As one walks through retirement villages, it becomes readily apparent that there are many seniors involved with tennis and other activities that earlier were relegated solely to younger players. Due to better nutrition and improved physical exercise we are not only living significantly longer, we seem to be aging better, perhaps even more slowly.

I have participated in an accommodation sport especially designed for older adults. When I was younger I played tennis. I had a particular partner with whom I was fairly evenly matched and we enjoyed playing each other competitively for many hours at a time. As the years went on and covering the whole court became more difficult, I began to partner up and play doubles. Later still, as I increased my stamina by jogging for half-marathon distances, I sought out a more taxing sport requiring more intensity but less ground to cover and I discovered racquetball. After two decades of twice-weekly workouts on the racquetball courts, various nagging injuries told me it was time to quit. A fractured right femur due to a bicycle accident and subsequent hip replacement surgery suspended my athletic endeavors for a number of years until I discovered a relatively new sport called pickleball.

Pickleball is a game played on a modified miniature tennis court, which combines some of the aspects of court and table tennis (ping pong). Like with those two sports, the two sides are separated by a net, with line-demarcated courts on each side. The balls are modified wiffle balls. When played with the gusto of heated competition the game gives a good workout. When playing doubles with a partner, one is required to only cover a rectangular area 10 feet wide, and therefore this game is well-suited to the abilities of older athletes. Due to the size of the court and rule restrictions, seniors can be quite competitive with younger players. From personal experience, there is nothing as gratifying as being over eighty years old and beating a young man of twenty-three at any game.

It's an ego booster. There are retirement communities throughout the country with a growing number of pickleball courts and players. I can highly recommend it for anyone physically fit enough to play. It is a wonderful way to get a workout and it's a lot of fun. It is also a good invitation to form new friends as well as playmates. Being teammates in rotating doubles and mixed doubles games leads easily to social engagements and friendships. It has become one of the fastest growing sports.[24]

RELOCATION

If your retirement plans include moving to a new home, there are many changes that may have to be made. The best way to handle this is to delay the real estate closing on any property sold or purchased to allow sufficient time to sort out all the items you wish to keep and which to discard. This is particularly true, as is the case with most retirees, when moving from a large home to a smaller one. If you have lived in your house for a long time, many things have piled up. Closets, attics and basements tend to accumulate items, some at one time cherished and perhaps long forgotten. It is important that you do not rush or allow some real estate agent to pressure you in his or her haste to make a sale. Take your time deciding what you want to take with you and what you may choose to give away to family members or friends. If you have some items that might have value that you no longer wish to keep, you can have yard sales. If you have furniture or art pieces that just won't fit into your new home or apartment, you can have an open house sale. If you don't feel comfortable or believe you don't have the expertise to price the items correctly and don't mind sharing the profits, there are professionals you can hire to sell your household items for you.

Whatever you do, don't rush. Although some realtors will tell you that the first offer you receive on your home will usually be the best and this may be true, I believe it is prudent to place your home on the market at a price higher than what the realtors suggest. The real estate agents know the market, but they are also in business to make a sale as soon as possible. What the agents don't know is if there is a buyer out there who may be willing to pay more if they really want the property. This is particularly true with young first-time buyers who may fall in love with a place and, if they can afford it, are willing to overpay. Don't let a salesperson influence you into undervaluing your home. I feel that in any ensuing negotiation you can always come down in price, but it's very difficult to come back up.

Besides financial and physical preparations for retired life, the social and spiritual aspects have to be attended to as well. Make sure you are relocating to a situation that is truly the best for you in every way and not just an attempt at wish-fulfillment.

As a young man I always dreamed of owning a boat large enough to live on in retirement and my wife and I even thought about selling our house, buying a boat and trying to see if we would enjoy living like that. My wife, being more practical than I am, suggested that we charter a boat run by a husband-and-wife team first, to see how it worked out for them. The couple had been in business together, the wife became ill and could no longer stand the pressure of catering to many clients and, as the husband had always wanted to pursue a venture including his love of water, they sold their business, took the proceeds and had a boat specially made for chartering.

One of the most pleasurable vacations I have enjoyed was to charter a boat, cruise the Sir Francis Drake Channel and visit the British Virgin Islands. You will see beautiful scenery, enjoy a delightful climate and swim and snorkel in the bluest water imaginable. This is delightful if you are on someone else's boat or a cruise ship, but it can be just a hard job if you are the boat owner. From day one of the cruise it became apparent that to enjoy life as a large boat owner you must become a master mechanic or you have to hire a crew to do it for you. Although the boat was relatively new, each day something stopped functioning properly. First the desalinator (a machine which removes salt and other minerals from salt water) stopped working, so we had no water to drink and had to make an unscheduled port stop to make repairs. Next the water pump malfunctioned. Luckily the captain had a spare on board and was able to replace it himself. It seemed each day new repairs had to be made. Although we had a wonderful vacation, after one week aboard I knew this was not the way I wanted to spend my time after retirement. The dream of many years proved to be an unrealistic illusion.

If you harbor some fanciful wish, such as running a bed and breakfast or owning a bar after you leave your day job, try it out before you buy. Make sure it's really what you were cut out to do. Don't just plunge ahead on the idea this is what was meant to be. Like me, you may be unpleasantly surprised and disappointed.

Remember that the home you purchase in which to spend your retirement years may very well be the last house you will ever own, so make sure it has all the comfortable things you desire in it. Also make sure it's near enough to those people and places you want or need to visit, like family, doctors and spiritual advisers.

MEDICAL CARE

Older adults have more ailments and, on average, need to take more medications than younger folks. It is therefore absolutely necessary to have good medical care available and a handy pharmacy, preferably one open twenty-four hours a day. There has been publicity luring poorer people to consider moving outside the United States to live in foreign countries, such as in Latin America, where real estate and the cost of living is considerably cheaper. My wife and I once considered buying a home or a condominium on a semi-tropical island. The weather and ocean views were extremely inviting, but the local medical care was nowhere near what we take for granted in this country and so we decided against it. If one of us had a medical emergency, we would have had to be flown by a chartered plane to the nearest hospital. If the condition was very serious, then the chances for survival would have been much less than if the illness occurred in the United States. This, coupled with the question of security, made us decide against living in another country. For adventurous folks wanting a better life, it can be an option.

The diseases more prevalent in the older population are different from those prevalent in younger people. Body responses to environmental factors and medications also change with the aging process. Therefore, as you get into retirement age, whenever possible you should come under the care of a physician with expertise in geriatric medicine.

While there are many illnesses which can be life threatening in both young and old, like heart disease and stroke, the disease most identified with the elderly is dementia. Over five million Americans suffer with Alzheimer's disease, which is the most common diagnosis used in this country for non-traumatic dementias. This is projected to grow to fifty million by 2050. It is currently reported that it is the sixth-leading cause of death in the United States. In the March 6, 2013, issue of the journal *Neurology* it was written that a study showed that Alzheimer's disease may be greatly underreported and could actually be the third-leading cause of mortality in this country.[25] According to Alzheimer's Disease International, as of 2013, there were an estimated 44.4 million people with Alzheimer's worldwide and this number will increase to an estimated 75.6 million by 2030. Much of this increase will occur in developing countries, where 62 percent of people with dementia live. The elderly population is growing most rapidly in China and India, as well as many South Asian and

Western Pacific countries. Since many people are now living longer and healthier lives, the world population has a greater proportion of older people.[26] Dementia mainly affects older people and thus there are more people with dementia.

Despite claims to the contrary by some drug manufacturers of the efficacy of their products' ability to diminish the severity of symptoms in mild-to-moderate cases, there are no medicines currently available which have a clinically significant effect on the disease. In my three decades as a consultant to various geriatric treatment facilities, I never saw a noticeable improvement in an Alzheimer's patient using the available medicines. There have been hundreds of attempts to develop an effective drug for Alzheimer's disease and all have failed.

The symptoms of dementia are progressive and debilitating. While all people become forgetful as they age, the memory loss associated with Alzheimer's disease and related dementias is much more pronounced and eventually grows to interfere with adequate cognitive functioning. Motor function and coordinating abilities decline and routine tasks become more and more difficult to do, until the basic activities of autonomous living require aid. A definite indication of the onset of dementia is the symptom of disorientation, like getting lost trying to find a location that the person had gone to many times before.

Dementia patients often exhibit a marked change in personality, such as changing from being a passive, easygoing person to being aggressive, confrontational and even disruptive in public. As the dementia grows, psychotic-like symptoms like paranoia may be evident. The patient may become suspicious of anyone in contact with him or her and be accusatory. As the disease progresses, the dementia patient becomes disorganized and can no longer plan daily activities as before. Routine tasks, like going to the grocery store, become unmanageable. Very often the inability to perform leads to frustration and agitation with outbursts of anger. More serious are psychotic-like symptoms like hallucinations and delusions, wherein the demented patient is tormented by seeing visions no one else can see or hearing voices no one else hears. These symptoms often become so severe that the patient's safety and that of others is in danger, so they require treatment with powerful antipsychotic medications which have potential side effects that can increase confusion and complicate the syndrome even more. Dementia patients have been known to become sexually aggressive and act out inappropriately in public. They may revert to infantile behavior and abruptly remove their clothing or masturbate in front of others. Nursing home personnel are usually schooled to be on the watch to stop demented sexual predators from molesting other defenseless dementia patients. The cognitive decline advances so that reasoning ability, thinking, reading and retaining information, problem solving, language and speech are progressively compromised.

Dementia is a debilitating disease which, when it afflicts one of a pair of retirees, can disrupt retirement plans and thrust the other partner into the role of caregiver. On many occasions this has proven to be a difficult job which has overwhelmed the caregiver. Those who physically or emotionally could not cope with changing diapers, treating bedsores, putting up with abusive outbursts and living with a person who no longer is what they once were, place the dementia patient into a nursing home even while beset by guilt over abandoning a loved one. Many times this is a family decision when it becomes obvious that the caregiver is besieged and exhausted and can no longer carry this burden. Some people have the strength of body and character to deliver loving care for years, keeping their loved ones at home. Some Alzheimer's patients linger on for years, gradually deteriorating. Other caregivers, cast into this difficult role, simply cannot cope with the demands of providing of adequate responses to the day-to-day requirements of their mentally and physically ill partners.

Alzheimer's disease has been studied intently for many years but its causes, best treatment and cure have eluded researchers. Many consider it to be like many cancers—not one disease but a confluence of diseases. Under microscopic analysis, amyloid or tau protein clumps found in the brain have been associated with the disease but drugs that reduce these have failed to be of any value in stopping the cognitive decline. Since many people having such brain abnormalities (found on autopsies) never developed dementia, the research community has reached the conclusion that just finding better drugs to target the toxic proteins is not enough to adequately fight the disease. Genetic research is holding out hope for advanced treatment discoveries in fighting disabling brain disorders like Parkinson's disease. Direction in Alzheimer's disease research may be turning to the investigation of the brain's innate neuroprotective gene-regulating proteins. Studying proteins, present from birth, which suppress genes involved in cell death that may be involved in the progression of Alzheimer's disease could lead to a new family of chemical agents capable of more effectively slowing the onslaught of this debilitating disease. Unfortunately, the widespread availability of such drugs is probably years away.

Deciding to place a loved one whose partner cannot give adequate care in a nursing home for long-term care is a gut-wrenching decision to have to make and should be done after careful family deliberation. Although there are fine nursing facilities available, there are some which give only minimally-acceptable care. As someone who has spent many hours in the rooms of debilitated patients, my advice if you need to choose a nursing home is to check it out carefully. Visit as many areas of the home as possible. Inquire as to the treatment facilities and medical care available. Speak to as many members of the nursing staff and responsive residents as you can so you can make an informed decision on the working conditions and the care received from the patients' points of view. Ask for recommendations from other people who have placed family members in such institutions. Do not settle on the first nursing home you visit, although it seems nice and may ultimately prove to be the best one that you will see. Measure a facility by what you would want for yourself. Would you want to spend what may be the last days of your life in a place like this?

I have seen many spouses reluctantly place a loved retiree, either for an incurable physical or mental disorder, in a nursing home and then, out of guilt or love, become a regular visitor. They feel compelled to return, sometimes each day or several times a day if they live nearby, making the daily pilgrimage their way of life. While such devotion may be seen as admirable by many, in some cases it can be self-destructive, as when the compulsion to visit is seen as a curse and resentment builds up against the sick spouse. They may feel that the last years are being stolen by a travesty not of one's making or choosing. Comparing one's miserable lot to others who seem to be enjoying their retired lives can turn love into hate and the hidden wish that the spouse should die so that life can have meaning again. Sensing this, many patients feed off the vibes coming their way, becoming more depressed and also wishing for their death to come soon.

MODERATION

All things should be anticipated with a sense of moderation. Preparing thoroughly for retirement requires preparing for the worst as well as the best. By all means, live life to the fullest but remember we all die in the end. As noted before, serious illnesses like Parkinson's, Alzheimer's, debilitating strokes and cancers can destroy fragile relationships and retirement plans. Besides financial and practical preparation for disasters, there has to be rational psychological anticipation. No one looks forward to dying but the party has to end sometime and being prepared for calamity is half the battle of acceptance. Once again, knowing yourself, your tolerance for pain, the strength of your relationship and the vulnerability of your partner are vital in meeting the end with the strength and serenity to go on with dignity.

FAILED RETIREMENT

Some attempts at retirement do not succeed. Either due to poor planning, changed external factors or boredom, miscalculations doom the retirement attempt. Some people just can't thrive in a retirement environment. Others may find that with the added free time, they or their spouses actually spend more money than before, can no longer make ends meet and have to go back to some kind of gainful employment.

On occasion I have come across a retired couple who have reached the conclusion that their marriage could not survive retirement. The husband usually was involved in an occupation, like the military, which kept him away from home much of the time, rarely being involved with bringing up the children or making day-to-day household decisions. Although they were still involved with each other, this chronic separation, with increased allocation of family decision making placed mostly on the wife, created a sense of division of responsibilities which became greatly altered when the husband began to stay home. Some spouses can overcome this adjustment period but other marriages cannot survive the competition for dominance that may ensue. The anticipated loss of a position of power felt to be earned and deserved can test any relationship.

This disruption is not as traumatic as the difficulties encountered by those with partners returning from war with Post-Traumatic Stress Disorder, exhibiting antisocial behavior. PTSD is usually a disruptive problem straining young marriages, while the problem of reunification of a marriage conducted mainly from afar presents a challenge for older retirees. This personality clash has resulted in an upswing in the divorce rate among people married for over twenty years. Much time apart allows the onset of loneliness and the meeting of other suitable lovers, which can endanger even stable mature marriages. Marital infidelity is a problem across the country.

Marital stability must be a consideration when planning retirement. A marriage with a history of separations, marred by suspected or proven infidelities on the part of one or both partners, can be a very fragile basis for a lasting, fulfilling retirement. This is more pertinent when there are insufficient funds to support both partners living separately. If the pair go even further and make it a legal issue, the legal fees can, in some cases, completely destroy any retirement possibilities.

The opposite situation also presents a problem: People who stay together bound by a financial or dependency need in a non-satisfying marriage need to overcome their fear of the alternative. To paraphrase an old saying, "It's better to live with the devil you know than to seek out the devil you don't know, who may turn out to be worse." If you can't abide the attitude and behavior of someone you only experience occasionally as you are both involved in two different life experiences, what happens when you are thrust into daily closeness? Can you accommodate that need to be apart and continue an existence of separate emotional lives in retirement, or will you discover a new avenue of closeness to bind you together, as when you were first attracted to each other? This emotional awareness and preparation is required to intelligently proceed into the retirement years.

In my years of practicing marital counseling I have seen marriages challenged by many different precipitants. Some were grave and truly disturbing, but others seem trivial in retrospect. A great deal of the problem began long before the marriage was consummated, when the partners were indoctrinated by their families, friends and the media with the idea of a blissful prince-and-princess courtship and paradise thereafter. Marriage is a serious adult affair. Unfortunately, too many children play the game. Many get married for the wrong reasons, to please their families, for fear of not being like their friends, for financial security and a host of other reasons. When seeking out a mate, the question that should always be asked is, "Can I see myself spending the rest of my life with this person?" Beauty fades with time; kindness of spirit and generosity do not.

Marital failure and dissolution at a younger age can be bothersome and troubling but at retirement it can be devastating. Every precaution should be taken to avoid it.

For couples with age differences, one spouse may not be ready to retire when the older counterpart is, so they may have difficulty in adjusting to the difference between their two positions in life. It is practical to wait until both pension plans are fully funded, but this may require the one ready to retire to delay plans long anticipated. Role reversals can lead to added frustration, as can childrearing in December-May relationships. The excitement of a new beginning with a partner of a much lesser age, bringing back youthful memories and a chance for a second or third attempt to recapture romance, may pale when brought up against the realities of the restrictions of that younger age, when the desire for the freedom of a retired state emerges. In your seventies it may not be as easy to be kept up night after night, as it was in your thirties, by a screaming infant.

A fulfilling marriage needs two partners and, when one partner is ready to retire and the other one is not, one has to accommodate the other to continue in a harmonious union. This requires patience and understanding on both sides, with mutual admiration and respect. So when one spouse is away at a business conference for three days and the retired one has to carry on the household chores alone, or conversely when the retired one is off on a hunting trip leaving the other spouse alone, no recrimination should be forthcoming. Each has to respect the other's position and outlook.

This attempt to reconcile two different perspectives and unify two different levels of existence is not easy and requires effort and mutual reassurance. One couple who has done this quite successfully is an example: Tom was a high school teacher and basketball coach who was required to take early retirement while still in his fifties, because of school budget cutbacks. His wife Jayne is a nurse at a regional hospital. She is still years away from having funded an adequate retirement package. She goes to work each day while he stays home and cares for the house and family. When the weather allows, he plays golf three times a week and is on the indoor pickleball courts the other two afternoons, all year long. It works for them because of their teamwork and because of the faith and trust they have in each other.

Many of the problems of modern marriages are founded in an erosion of the faith and trust we have in each other and our fellow human beings in general. With the spread of social media, our privacy has been stripped away, exposing our adolescent risk-taking to new extremes. It has become a greater age of narcissistic prominence than in the recent past. Many of us have lost the ability to love unconditionally, since we don't need to give a part of ourselves away anymore. As we become more self-sufficient, we don't need to rely on another as in years gone by and need is a big part of love. Love has become a more relegated commodity, used for purposes other than devotion. As we live longer, it's harder to make love last. We have to keep nurturing it, keep feeding it in new ways, keep trying.

As atrocities around the world are made evident daily through worldwide media coverage, it cannot escape the young that we live in a time when the darkest side of humanity is on display. What has happened to the soul of mankind? Are we teetering on the rim of Dante's hellpit? It sometimes seems so. The more we gain individuality, as we seek greater and greater freedom of expression, the more interpersonal relationships seem to become superficial. Deep, meaningful love of another is a victim in this age of widespread self-gratification.

One of the ways to express a deep empathy for others is to show compassion and generosity in times of need. Love can be expressed through companionship and being attentive to the desires of another.

VOLUNTEERISM

One of the questions most often asked by those skeptical about whether retirement is right for them is, "What will I do after I retire, since I really don't have any hobbies?" One answer is to teach others, help others and give back to your community. If you have acquired a skill which is no longer marketable because of your age, volunteer your time to teach younger people to be able to better support themselves. If you know of a mentoring program in your area, volunteer your time to help some disadvantaged young person to keep away from a lawless existence. You have life experience which is valuable to someone who may not have had a strong parental figure to guide him or her. There are community services always asking for senior citizens to donate their time and efforts for worthwhile causes.

Helene, a retired schoolteacher, had been very devoted to teaching. She used to spend many hours after school, after her own children were grown and had moved away, tutoring students. After Helene and her husband retired, she found that she missed the classroom atmosphere and doing something that she loved and felt she was good at. After giving it much thought, she began to tutor immigrants wanting to take the exam to become American citizens. On the days she wasn't doing that, she and her husband volunteered to serve meals at a soup kitchen. The pride she felt in helping the needy adequately replaced the loss of the job to which she had been devoted. The feeling that she was again doing important work sustained the self-image that she had built up over the years.

This self-image, or ego, is what we think of ourselves. It is the esteem we hold ourselves in. It makes us what we are. It chooses what we do. It is our very essence. It is vital for us to be proud of ourselves and what we have accomplished, for in the final analysis, we are alone in this animal shell we call the body. We are alone in our thoughts. We are the final judge and jury of our destiny, whether to be our own best friend or worst enemy. We make the decisions that shape our lives in accomplishment or destruction. We are the ones who fight our demons or give in to them. We revel in victory and are gloomy in perceived defeat. It's so important to be proud of oneself at life's end, for without this self-appreciation we have to admit having wasted the most precious gift of all—the gift of life.

Be as good and generous to yourself as possible, so that you can pass this on to others, because in the final analysis you tend to treat others like you treat yourself. Preparing adequately for a comfortable retirement is being good to yourself. It means you won't have to be a burden to anyone else. It means you have provided adequately for your loved ones and made it possible for them to be independent and self-sufficient. By your example you have passed this lesson on for generations to come. This applies to all avenues of preparation: psychological, practical and financial.

A most disturbing worry of old age is outliving your money and dying destitute. Some of the most famous and brilliant people in history lost their money and suffered. The genius of Thomas Jefferson could not keep him from overspending and losing his home. The patriot Thomas Paine and the philosopher Rousseau died in poverty. Many watched the televised account in disbelief as a former Secretary of the Treasury, John Connally, had to sell his home furnishings to satisfy his bankruptcy because of poor business decisions.

To prevent American workers from meeting such a fate, the Social Security Act of 1935 was instituted during the Great Depression.

WORKING IN RETIREMENT

While many people envision the ideal retirement scene to feature relaxing in a lounge chair beside a pool sipping a favorite beverage, others want to experience their long-cherished dream job. Go to malls, factories and offices. Make inquiries and you will be surprised to find how many workers who feel frustrated in their current jobs want to continue working after retirement at something they really would love to do. It is a great blessing to make your living by doing something you love and might do even if you didn't need the money. Thousands of employees around the country who are uninspired by the jobs in which they have been trapped are just waiting for the time when they are free enough and financially secure enough to follow their dreams, the point when they will no longer have to work at unfulfilling jobs.

Retirement may offer an opportunity to begin anew. Time would be available to seek out new educational aid or perhaps to retrain. If at all possible, you should begin that education or retraining program after working hours while you are still at your current job, so you can begin your new career as soon as you leave your old job. If you are unhappy with your financial status after retiring, if you feel your pension or severance package is inadequate, this might be the perfect way to enhance your income and give yourself the lifestyle you want.

There are many stories about law enforcement officers who go into security work or become private investigators after leaving the police force and also about surgeons, who can no longer operate, who go into hospital or insurance administration. For those who want or need to continue working, it is best to plan ahead and lay the foundation while still working at the original job. Try to set enough money aside to start. Find out if adequate financing is available for a new venture. Make sure you have the money and information to proceed. Don't buy a restaurant, because your friends have all told you that you are a great cook, before you have learned about the food business. Get adequate training first and seek out expert advice. Find a business adviser to help you formulate a business plan. If you want to become involved in farming or another business requiring the use of heavy equipment, make sure you are adequately insured. For example, you will need healthcare, disability and even long-term care insurance. You need to protect your wealth against unexpected catastrophes; otherwise, you are placing your entire future and that of your dependents in jeopardy.

New careers make new demands on your time, may determine your place of residence and your financial choices. If after retiring from your old job you decide to open a retail store, you may find it more difficult than a younger person to get a business loan, because the bank officer may decide that you don't have as many years to pay off the loan. The obstacles to an easy second career may be varied, depending on your choice, but the adventure of attempting to succeed in a new work experience at an advanced age might be worth the risk for those who did not get the pleasure they wanted the first time around.

SOCIAL SECURITY

The recent recession of the first decade of the twenty-first century was brought on by the marketing of derivatives, bundles of mortgages which were sold as bonds by banking institutions. After thousands of years of people renting from landlords, it became unwise government policy to facilitate home ownership by people who could not afford to pay off the mortgages that the banks rushed to sell in order to maximize their profits. Home ownership, the American dream, was traditionally available only to those who were able to provide a 10 to 20 percent down payment. The government facilitation was implemented by the repeal of the Glass-Steagall Act of 1932. The Glass-Steagall Act was placed into law because the stock market crash of the 1920s was brought on by the ready availability of margin buying on the stock exchange. People could borrow freely from the commercial aspect of a bank to purchase equities from the investment portion of that bank. The Glass-Steagall Act separated commercial from investment banking to prevent this from happening again. Not learning from the mistake of the first Great Depression, in the last decade of the twentieth century the government repealed Glass-Steagall, which allowed banks to buy brokerage firms and sell their groups of bad mortgages for market purchase. With large-scale default on these mortgages, many banks fell into financial difficulty, requiring a government bailout. Some banking institutions which did not qualify for government aid were allowed to fail.

Many investors suffered greatly as stock markets fell sharply. Businesses declined and many lost their jobs. However, while things were bad as unemployment skyrocketed to 12 percent at the height of the recession, it was much less damaging than the 25 percent unemployment in the 1930s. Legislation like unemployment insurance and Social Security was implemented because of the catastrophe of the Great Depression and helped mitigate the financial losses this time.

One of the important decisions to be made near the time of retirement is when to begin receiving Social Security payments. For many retirees, especially those who have not adequately prepared, Social Security income will be the financial cornerstone of their retirement benefits. For those who need the money, there is little choice. Nearly half of Americans choose to receive their Social Security checks at the minimum allowable age of sixty-two. Some may not have dire need of the money but have been made aware of statistics that seem to suggest that in aggregate, antici-pating an average lifespan, the earlier that payments are begun, the greater the total received will be over the years. Since Social Security benefits are taxed like other income, this has not deterred people in lower tax brackets from electing to take their Social Security benefits at age sixty-two.

No one can argue with people choosing to receive money when they need it, especially when the government will take little (or even none in the lowest income level) back in taxes. However, I advise the more affluent retirees or people who are working through retirement who don't need the money to wait as long as they can, until they need or are required at age seventy to receive their Social Security payments.

Why advise people to wait as long as possible to get money back from the government that has been paid for through regular Social Security deductions over the years? Because each year that is delayed in receiving Social Security payments adds 8 percent, so that the difference in the size of the annual amount if the indi-vidual begins to draw at age seventy is over 60 percent more than if they were taken at age sixty-two. At age seventy you receive about 40 percent more than at age sixty-five, one-third more than at age sixty-six and one quarter more than at age sixty-seven. So it makes sense that if you already have adequate income in your early six-ties and do not require additional funds, which may even push you into a higher tax bracket, to wait until you are seventy years old before starting to receive your Social Security payments.

Stephanie, a financial adviser, had as a client a schoolteacher who retired at age fifty-nine. She taught in a school district with a generous pension plan but felt she wanted to continue working and so she got a job as a real estate agent. Soon she was making more money at her new job than she used to make at her old one. At age sixty-five she decided that since she was doing so well at a job she enjoyed, she would work for another five years. She figured that since all of the females in her family lived until their late eighties and some even into their nineties, that there was a good chance she would also live a long time and could still enjoy retirement after age seventy. She enjoyed interacting with adults at work after many years dealing with children. As she was now a widow living alone in a condominium which she owned with no mortgage to pay, she really didn't need additional income. Still, Stephanie wanted to receive her Social Security benefits at age sixty-five. Her financial consultant advised that she wait until age seventy. She initially resisted, stating that she was entitled to receive this money she had paid in over many years. At first she was quite adamant that she should begin getting the money at age sixty-five. However, after the financial adviser explained to her that the income would only add to her tax bill, as well as pointing out that she didn't need it yet and would receive 40 percent more at age seventy, she rethought her options.

Since people, on average, are living longer, there is much legislative pressure in America to increase the age when people will be eligible to receive Social Security benefits. The nominal sixty-five-year retirement standard was instituted when the average age expectancy was less than seventy and Social Security benefits, on average, were counted on to last only a few years. Since we live much longer now and benefits may be received for many years, there is constant agitation in Washington, D.C., that the Social Security system will go broke if the standard retirement age is not readjusted to age seventy and eventually beyond, as the population continues to get older. It is therefore prudent for younger workers, wise enough to be planning seriously for retirement, to take into consideration the possibility that there will be legislation passed sometime in the future that will mean they will not be able to receive Social Security benefits until an older age than what is available for today's seniors.

Although Social Security benefits alone usually cannot fund an adequate retirement as per the formula requirements stated in this book, they do constitute an annuity-like basis for retirement income. Many older adults who were not wise enough to save or never earned enough money to be able to save and had to retire on Social Security benefits alone are living meager existences, surviving from month to month. That is why it is so important that workers maximize their contributions to their retirement plans while they can.

Growing old and poor is a difficult, unhappy process. Remember, while money only buys love in a pet store, it can buy comfort. Money does pay the bills and keeps the bill collectors from hounding you. As much as there are those in our society who decry greed and avarice, the pursuit of the almighty buck puts our kids through college and pays the rent or mortgage. Without money we are destitute and burdens on society. In a capitalistic country it is our responsibility to earn as much as we legally can to remain independent and take care of our needs and of those who depend on us and put away a sufficient amount to be able to fund the standard of retirement living we deserve.

CHAPTER 10

Occupying Yourself in Retirement

Whenever I'm around one group of my friends, almost all of whom feel they never will retire, invariably the question of what I do with myself during the course of each day gets asked. These men are mostly professionals, lawyers, doctors, dentists; one is in real estate, another owns a travel agency. They all profess having no important hobbies; they don't play golf, they don't fish, but they are enthusiastic fans of local sports teams. They go to the stadiums to watch the professional athletes play and some even have season tickets. Most go to the theater to see plays and movies and a few enjoy the opera. What they all have in common is that they are closely tied to their families and communities. They all wish to live close to their children and grandchildren. They also require the cultural opportunities found only in a large urban setting. Most live in the city of their birth and although several have a second home, they use it only sparingly as a vacation spot. Their wives either work with their husbands or spend much of their time helping out the mothers of their grandchildren. Some are involved with religious organizations.

In the group, I am not the only retiree. There is one other named Tate and he may have soured some of these other friends on retirement. He practiced gynecology until a bad case of spinal stenosis made it impossible for him to continue, so he sold his practice and retired underfunded (by the formulas of this book) much too early, at age fifty-eight. Although he was an able investor, he did take a financial beating in the recent recession. Being financially pinched, he was forced to sell the house he and his wife had lived in for many years and moved into a retirement community far out in the suburbs, where the prices were much more reasonable. Whenever the friends meet, his example of having to live at a much lower level after retirement reinforces the fear present in all the others of having to sacrifice their living standards after retirement.

In answering the question about what I do with myself each day, I usually begin by telling people that since I've retired it seems as if there aren't enough hours in the day for me to accomplish what I set out to do each morning. To start with, I've always been of the opinion that uninterrupted sleep is very important for mental health. I try to get at least eight hours of sleep a night. I have never used an alarm clock that I can remember. I feel that being rudely awakened is a shock to the system and interrupts a necessary bodily function, which cannot be adequately made up later on. Sufficient sleep has been shown to improve both physical and mental activity. Adequate sleep translates to better grades in school and has been proven to facilitate better performance on the playing field. Whenever I need to get up earlier than usual, I go to sleep that many hours earlier and I very rarely require awakening to be on time.

Many of you reading this would respond dubiously with, "Try doing that with young children around." I tried by sleeping with a pillow over my head and allocating nighttime child care to my wife as she worked at home, while I had to get up and go to the office. Nothing works 100 percent of the time. You just have to strive for perfection, knowing full well that you never will achieve it. Anyway, getting a full night's sleep is important and having the opportunity to do that is one of the blessings of retirement.

After getting up and brushing my teeth, I go to my exercise nook. One of the smartest things I've done is to have an exercise area close to my bedroom and bathroom. In all the houses where we have lived I have had some space right near where I sleep allocated for exercise equipment so I can literally tumble out of bed and be immediately reminded to work out first thing in the morning. For me this is important because I don't really love doing exercise and it is easy for me to get distracted and become involved in something else. Currently I have a stationary bicycle, an elliptical trainer and a full set of weights in the small alcove near my bed. I use the bike and the elliptical on alternate days and work out with the weights three days a week. To overcome the boredom of exercising alone I watch television while I work out. I have always had a television set in my exercise quarters. I usually catch the world and business news before I switch to a sports channel. I make my own breakfast after about two hours of exercise and news.

Along with adequate sleep at night, keeping to a healthy diet is also important to maintain good physical and mental health. I don't smoke and I have never tried recreational drugs. I never felt the need. Even before my medical days, I was aware that what you put in your body can lead to toxic results. I gave up smoking cigarettes over fifty years ago. I went cold turkey from two packs a day to none. I couldn't put up with the sore throats, so I had to stop smoking even before the first surgeon general's report about smoking leading to lung cancer. With the pressure of medical school I did drink regularly at fraternity parties but now, since alcoholic beverages give me heartburn, I rarely have a cocktail.

As for my diet, I shy away from "amine" containing foods and beverages. Everything containing a major component chemical ending in "*ine*" should be, in my opinion, avoided: caffeine (I don't drink coffee and only decaffeinated tea), codeine, etc., bad chemicals ending in *"ine"* to be avoided. I shy away from using much salt or sugar. In the senior years many people tend to have elevated blood pressure and it's a good idea to limit salt intake, even if you have normal blood pressure, as a preventive measure.

According to published statistics, almost 300 million people worldwide have diabetes. It is estimated to afflict up to one in every twenty or so inhabitants of the earth. About one and one-half million people die each year from this illness, making it one of the most lethal diseases. Although the most prevalent form is Type 2 or what was once called adult-onset diabetes (since the increase in childhood obesity it is being found in children now more than ever), there is an elderly-onset form which is first diagnosed in older people. Diabetes runs in families and is related to obesity and overindulgence in sugar and sugar-rich food. It has been reported that over 25 million Americans have been diagnosed with diabetes.[27]

I stopped using raw sugar as soon as sugar substitutes were reported to be relatively safe in medical literature. Still, I use these sugar substitutes with caution. Borrowing from an old pharmacological ploy, wherein medications with the same beneficial qualities but different side effects were combined in half doses to get the maximum positive results with lessened unwanted symptoms, I use half amounts of the saccharin-containing sweetener out of the pink packet with half amounts of the aspartame-containing sweetener out of the blue packet to sweeten my food and beverages. Thereby, if there are any bad side effects, as some claim there are from use of these artificial agents, I get a lessened exposure to each. In any case, I won't be increasing my chances of getting diabetes as might be the case with the use of sugar. Diabetes occurs as often in women as it does in men.

I have to admit I do sprinkle some artificial sweetener on my morning cereal. I enjoy whole-grain wheat flakes, which contain 100 percent of the daily requirements for just about all of the vitamins that, according to dietary experts, the body requires. They taste better when sweetened. They also have enough fiber in them to keep me going to the bathroom regularly. I look forward to breakfast each day as not only a hunger-satisfying meal but as an important event.

I continue to be concerned about diabetes, because to tell the truth I show very little resistance when I am around sweets. My wife jokes that is why I married her, because she is so sweet, and she is. A dear friend of mine, a lively physician who always made jokes and was quite a prankster, was a diabetic and never controlled his craving for sweet things. He continued to challenge his disease by giving in to his indulgences. He lost his battle and died in his early fifties. So I will use as much of the mixtures of artificial sweeteners as needed to satisfy my cravings and intake as little true sugar as I can get away with. It is a balance I can live with happily, as long as I can go on fooling my taste buds.

Breakfast time is special at our house. We all get to eat. I feed the fish and the dog gets to sink his teeth into his morning treat. My wife watches her favorite television programs and I read the newspaper. One of the great pleasures I enjoy, now having the time I didn't have before I retired, is to be able to really read the entire newspaper. I get a feeling of satisfaction in being made aware of not only the headline news you get in the visual media, but the in-depth reporting on various non-headline topics found in print. Keeping abreast of local news and cultural events makes me feel still in tune with the world I left behind in some measure. It is most important for older people not to experience being isolated from new technologies. I receive at least fifty or so e-mails each day and respond accordingly. We keep in touch with the doings of the younger generation via texting.

I was weaned off dairy foods by my gastroenterologist and enjoy having low-calorie almond milk with my cereal. Vanilla-flavored almond milk tastes better to me than regular milk. It also has less calories than skim milk and more calcium. Since I'm indoors a lot during the winter months, especially when I am writing, I don't get the sun exposure I should so I take calcium and vitamin D capsules. I'm wary of allowing any osteoporosis I may have to get worse. Twelve years ago I broke my hip during a bicycle accident and I only ride a stationary bike now. This fracture and resultant rehab interfered with my working schedule for five weeks and hastened my gradual retirement. I may have some toast and sugar-free blackberry preserves along with my cereal. My wife and I discuss our daily plans across the breakfast table. We also like to discuss world events.

In the warm weather I might go outside and work in my garden, raking in the fall and planting annuals in the spring. My garden is mostly a perennial garden of the English variety with several dozen kinds of roses. I used to have fancy tea roses, but they were vulnerable to diseases so I've settled on planting the hardier knock-out variety in recent years. Perennials don't bloom as intensely in the hot summer months, so I augment the color with flowering vincas and geraniums. The shady areas come alive with the pretty blooms of New Guinea impatiens. The fall is glorified by the second blooming of the roses and the prolific flowering of mums and Montauk daisies, as well as asters and hydrangeas, which can grow very tall.

I used to joke that the difference between working and being retired is that I could go fishing twice a week instead of just once a week. When the weather allows and the water is calm, there is nothing that relaxes me more than going out to sea. I have an old twenty-seven-foot fishing boat. My wife calls my boat my mistress. I bought the boat new thirty-five years ago and had to replace the two inboard engines ten years ago after many long hours of service. I don't care for bottom fishing, just sitting around and waiting for the stripers or flounders to bite. I prefer to troll in the ocean and watch the bluefish, sailfish or marlin jump or drag in a tuna. If I don't catch a fish that day, I can still appreciate having taken a mini-cruise. Being out on the ocean, with land far away, is like going out into space. It is an adventure.

It was almost fatal once. It was in the spring of 1980, the year Mount St. Helens erupted. On that bleak day I had just gotten my boat out of the marina where it was kept for winter storage. It was my initial outing of the boating season. I was no more than five miles outside of the inlet when I viewed something unusual. I was alone, checking out the boat's equipment. Later on I could only describe the scene as one in which the sky shrunk. As I realized that the boat was being approached by a rogue wave, I turned the boat's bow directly into the wave. When the wave hit, the boat was stood up on its stern and I was gazing at the sky, gripping the wheel at the helm with all my strength. I feared going overboard and being trapped beneath the hull. Fortunately the wave passed and the boat returned to its regular position. The water was diverted over my head by the windscreen and flowed out back through the self-bailing cockpit. However, the force of the water was so powerful that it snapped my two outrigger poles, which broke off at the level of their chrome sleeves. Understandably this was a harrowing experience, but one many seasoned boaters have endured. It left me respecting the power of the vast ocean as compared to my tiny craft as never before. However, I would not be deterred from returning again, because as frightening as the experience was, it was also exhilarating. I had survived the elements. Whenever I leave the dock now, I tell my wife that if perchance I should not return to place this epitaph on my gravestone: "He died at sea, where he wanted to be."

Whenever I have friends over to go fishing we plan to go out early in the morning. If I want to leave at 6 A.M., I usually go to bed around 9 P.M., no later than 10 P.M., so I can get a full night's sleep. When you bounce around in a small boat for many hours it's tiring at any age, but when you get older it helps to have had a good night's sleep before you start out.

When my torn rotator cuff and torn labrum in my right shoulder allow, I try to play pickleball. I used to play regularly two or three times a week before I tore my labrum and avulsed my glenohumeral ligament. The shoulder surgeon didn't think I required surgery, so I slaved away at physical therapy for about six months, until I was relatively pain free and had full mobility. I still don't have all the strength back in my right arm, but it is serviceable.

My wife loves being retired. Her passion is reading. She seems to devour a book every three or four days. When the weather allows, she plays mahjong once or twice a week with friends. Since her arthritis prevents her from lifting her arms high over her head, she goes each Friday to a hair salon to get her hair done, so she can look attractively coffed for our date night. It has become a ritual, since we have retired, that we go out every Friday night to a movie and eat dinner at a restaurant. It rekindles memories of the time when we were dating before we got married and it has special meaning for both of us.

In the afternoons when I'm not gardening, boating or playing pickleball, I write. While I was still working, I wrote a book, *The Judgment of J.D.*, based on my most interesting case, the psychoanalysis of a career criminal. After I retired, I devoted my study time to reading the greatest religious books available. I studied the Bible, the Koran and the books of other major religions intently. I also studied the great philosophers and their ideas about religion. In 2013 my second book, *The Newest Testament*, was published about the history and philosophy of religion.

There was a time just after I had retired that I had a great desire to paint pictures to hang on our walls. I was struck with the notion that our walls looked too bare and required adornment with artwork, so I began to paint. I always knew I could draw a little, but I never had a formal lesson, so I bought three books by noted art teachers on how to paint. At the art store where I bought my supplies, the clerk, an art major, talked me out of buying oil paints and steered me to acrylics. He said they would be easier to clean up, especially when using the glass palette he advised me to employ. I owe him thanks for making things easier.

I thrived on acrylics. I started out with simple subjects on small canvases but soon learned I needed larger areas to fully express myself. I began to copy photos of the many trips my family had taken to foreign lands. I used my love of water to paint silhouettes against the sea. Today our walls are replete with my renderings hanging alongside those of professional artists, some bought on vacation trips.

On occasion I may break to have a sandwich for lunch but many times I don't. Several times a day I interrupt working to check on how my stocks are doing. I have lived through enough downturns in the market to be very cautious about getting caught in a steep decline. It can be wise to set stop losses, so that stocks are sold if they fall to a certain dollar number.

When we are not out with family or friends, the dinner hour is our break from work or play. My wife and I watch our weight and we usually eat a light meal. I avoid red meat. My wife loves it but, knowing it can put on pounds, she rarely has it at home. She will order a steak at a restaurant. My wife loves salads but I find them unfulfilling. I make a great egg white omelet. I add turkey strips or turkey burger pieces and mushrooms or shrimp, depending on my mood. Sometimes I have smoked salmon on the side. The only fish my wife likes is canned tuna. I prefer salmon out of a can. The only bread we eat is thin-sliced whole wheat. The only cheese I eat is a soy substitute allowed on my no-dairy diet. I usually order seafood when we go out to eat. We both love Asian food, so we frequent local Chinese and Japanese restaurants, which also serve

Thai delights. Our food tastes are simple. One of our favorite eateries is a neighborhood tavern which serves great turkey burgers. We go there often with friends on Saturday nights and then watch a movie. We borrow Blu-ray discs from the school library down the street.

During the week, after-dinner time is family time at our house. I believe one reason my wife and I have enjoyed such a fulfilling relationship for so long is that we enjoy the same television programs, movies and sporting events. Outside of the daytime talk shows she watches, we just about always agree on which television dramas and action shows to watch together at night. We discuss which movies to watch on date night. We chose Friday, because that's usually the day on which new movies are shown for the first time in theaters. We almost always see eye-to-eye on the decisions we make, with some notable but not insurmountable exceptions.

One thing I love about my wife is that she is a great sports fan. I introduced her to sport fishing on our honeymoon. We were married the day after President Kennedy was assassinated. When I learned that JFK had caught a sailfish, had it taxidermied and hung it in the Oval Office, I told my wife that I would like to catch a big one and hang it over our living room couch. She said no at first, but changed her mind in the waters off Acapulco, Mexico. On her first fishing trip ever, she hooked a Pacific sailfish almost ten feet long, weighing over 120 pounds. When she saw the beautiful blue coloration of the regal creature as it was hauled onboard the fishing boat, she turned to me and said, "I think this would look nice on the wall over the sofa." It has hung in the living room of every home since.

When my wife and I were first married we moved into an apartment and proudly displayed the sailfish there with pictures of the catch and a plaque to denote the accomplishment. After our baby was born we moved into our first house. Getting the fish out of the eighteenth floor of the apartment building was quite a chore, as the crated fish did not fit into the elevator. The moving men had to take the elevator down to the floor below and place the crate on top of the elevator, and then take the elevator down to the basement level to be able to exit it through the street level lobby.

My wife became quite a fisherwoman after that episode. Unfortunately, my wife can't go fishing with me anymore. I miss this very much, especially when I see women on other boats. Most are younger and I am obliged to accept this, with great regret, along with the other disappointments of old age. My wife's companionship is one of the finest blessings of my life.

My wife and I watch baseball games on television in the summer, but enjoy them better when our favorite team has a chance to make the playoffs. As much as we like baseball, we are obsessed with football. We follow our teams' maneuvers during free agency and watch intently on draft day to learn which new players we have acquired. We come from a football-crazy family, calling each other to share the exhilaration of a victory or going over the mistakes of a costly defeat. Fall Sundays are reserved for watching football games, pre-game shows and postgame reviews. We both watch, entertained all day long.

Our evenings are spent sitting side-by-side in our swiveling rocking chairs, watching our favorite television programs until it is time to go to sleep. Every minute of every day is fully accounted for, without a moment of boredom or regret. I wish there were more hours in the day to enjoy this life. I like to imagine that things could improve, that all our pains would go away and we could go on like this indefinitely. But of course we can't. Mortality inevitably will curtail our experience of paradise.

Rather than being boring, I can assure my readers that retirement flies by faster and faster as time goes on. My wife and I laugh at how quickly each day passes. We just seem to turn around and it is Friday, our wonderful date night, again.

EPILOGUE

The formulas in this book have been the basis of a decade of my own retirement. I lived a middle-class professional existence and now have been able to luxuriate in the tranquil retirement of the past ten years.

I love being retired. In many ways it's the happiest time of my life. I feel fulfilled in having reached all my reasonable goals and these precious years of retirement are joyful on a par with carefree childhood. I wrote this book to share my experience with my readers and to teach any who would learn the formulas for a secure and prosperous retirement.

Read and reread this book and follow its precepts. It has worked for me; it can work for all of you.

Many things in life cannot be prepared for. We cannot prepare for events beyond our control, like unexpected illnesses or natural catastrophes. Even pleasant occurrences may happen by chance, yielding happy surprises. However, some things we can plan ahead for. We can anticipate certain needs, save for requirements and prepare for future events. One of the things we should anticipate from our earliest work years is the needs and attitudes of a successful retirement. While the future is in many cases beyond our control, it is vital to consider our future needs during the last years potentially allotted to us. Not doing this can lead to a later life of relative destitution and desperation.

It is the responsibility of every wage earner to put aside an adequate amount of money to take care of his or her retired years in a comfortable fashion and also to contribute to the well-being of those who depend upon him or her. Not doing this when one was able and perhaps becoming a burden on the community could be considered poor citizenship.

In bygone eras, when lifespans were much shorter and retirement considered a pleasure of the privileged few, there were many popular romantic notions about living for the moment, not caring about tomorrow and the worries it might bring. This was fine for yesteryear, when infectious diseases and environmental hazards were more prevalent and many futures appeared bleak. Despite the fact that with better dieting, sanitation and medical care we live much longer lives, in certain segments of the population similar ideas of sacrificing tomorrow for the immediate gratification of today is still quite prevalent.

This shortsightedness has left many in our current workforce facing a future under the so-called poverty line. As someone who grew up poor, I can tell you that while it is tolerable as a child, when your immediate contemporaries are in the same situation, facing poverty as an older adult, with the expected infirmities of the aging process, is not an enviable position. Anyone who is able to avoid this should do everything in his or her power to do so, even if it means foregoing some pleasures of the moment to afford the necessities of later on.

The most obvious basic step for young people to consider in preparing for a successful future is obtaining as much education as they can. All the studies I have seen tend to show that not only financial reward but also job satisfaction are usually directly related to the amount of education of the individual. College graduates make more than those with only a high school diploma and those with graduate degrees earn even more.

Of late there has been an alteration of status. Unfortunately, due to governmental and industrial funding and greater allocation to science rather than to the arts, many with degrees in underused areas have found difficulty in sustaining careers in their chosen fields of study. The technological revolution, just as the industrial revolution before it, has left many people in need of retraining and rethinking the nature of their future life's work. This is a repetition of what has occurred throughout history after new inventions. The automobile essentially did away with the need for blacksmiths to make horseshoes. Progress exerts a price on many. Just note the number of casualties in building our great bridges and digging our massive tunnels.

After gaining an adequate education, the graduate should obtain as good a job as his talent and qualifications afford him. He or she should then work diligently to advance in that chosen field. The greater the contribution, the greater the reward will be. The eye should always be on the future as well as the present, with mindfulness of a period when there might no longer be a time of work. This is something that can be prepared for with adequate planning on where to live, what to do, who to do it with and how to afford it all.

The key to a successful retirement is preparation, both emotional and financial, so that when the time comes to retire, the transition from work to a life of leisure will be easy and pleasant, in the proper place with as few financial worries as possible. This preparation should be begun as early as possible.

Above all else there are three basic components of an adequate preparation for retirement:

1. A PROPER PLACE TO LIVE
   A residence has to be chosen where one can realize
   cherished desires, a place where one feels at peace and yet
   has the freedom to continue growing as an individual, a
   place which allows stimulating contact and interaction with

interested and interesting other individuals, a place
which is conducive to the exploration of the cravings of
the inner mind.

2. SECURITY
There should be an accumulation of adequate wealth to
assure being able to afford all that is required for comfort
and joy. As no one is privy to their own date of debility or
demise, calculations for the amounts required should leave
a margin for unexpected longevity. To outlive your money
when you are most frail and unemployable should be viewed
as a disaster to be avoided by all means available.

3. SUPPORT
It is most important to continue being in close contact with
those who are important to you and those who consider you
important to them. The older one gets, the greater the value
of family and friends becomes. No matter whatever fame
and fortune one achieves, when nearing the end of life's
journey the only relationships that really count are those of
a loving family and true friendship. There has to be careful
consideration of the creation of adequate surroundings
when choosing proximity to those whom we love. It is
easier today to stay in touch with the availability of social
media and the like, even when living far apart, but constant
contact is important to maintain the bond of kinship. We
can never overestimate the importance of having people we
can rely on for proper support in a time of need.

As nutritional and both preventive and curative medical
sciences progress and the years of life are increased, more and
more people will join the ranks of retirees. Many of these tend to
migrate to balmier climates, as evidenced by the greatest population growth of the United States occurring in the southern region

of the country. With the aging of the population, retirement will be on the minds of a majority of people and they will seek guidance to obtain as good a retirement result as possible.

Many of the developed nations of Europe and also Japan are showing zero percent population growth with an aging citizenry. It is therefore important that people, even those enjoying the benefits of socialized programs, be individually responsible, at least in part, for their retirement finances, lest these governments become overwhelmed with the financial burden of caring for a majority of their citizens. The resultant increased taxation on following generations will contribute to financial crises, as we have recently experienced.

Therefore, the words of this book not only have financial implications for many but also bear sociological, political and psychological information that is important for those who have interest in such matters.

I leave the reader with this advice:

Adopt the emotional modalities and utilize the financial formulas outlined in this book and you will be better prepared to enjoy a successful retirement.

BIBLIOGRAPHY

Birren, James, Henry Imus, and William Windle, eds. *The Process of Aging in the Nervous System*. Springfield, Ill: Charles C. Thomas, 1959.

Graham, Benjamin. *Security Analysis*. New York: McGraw-Hill, 2004.

Hawkins, David. *Power vs. Force: The Hidden Determinants of Human Behavior*. Carlsbad, Ca: Hay House, 2002.

Houston, Paul, and Stephen Sokolow. *The Wise Leader: Doing the Right Things for the Right Reasons*. Bloomington, In: iUniverse, 2013.

Kubler-Ross, Elizabeth. *On Death and Dying*. New York: Scribner, 1969.

Safire, William. *Lend Me Your Ears: Great Speeches In History*. New York: Norton, 2004.

Schlossberg, Nancy. *Revitalizing Retirement: Reshaping Your Identity, Relationships, and Purpose*. Washington, DC: American Psychological Association, 2009.

Stanley, Thomas, and William Danko. *The Millionaire Next Door: The Surprising Secrets of America's Wealthy*. Atlanta, Ga: Longstreet Press, 1995.

Treen, Doug. *Psychology of Executive Retirement from Fear to Passion: Escape the Rat Race and Save Your Life*. Bloomington, In: iUniverse, 2009.

Wechsberg, Joseph. *The Merchant Bankers*. New York: Simon & Schuster, 1966.

NOTES

1. Tenzin Gyatso, the 14th Dalai Lama, *Dzogchen*. (Ithaca, NY: Snow Lion Publications, 2009).

2. Bob Harig, "Hagen paved the way for professional golfers," ESPN.com, August 11, 2005, http://sports.espn.go.com/golf/pgachampionship05/columns/story?id=2129495.

3. Martin B. Goldstein, *The Newest Testament*. (Bloomington, IN: Archway Publishing, 2013).

4. Ibid.

5. Virginia P. Reno and Joni I. Lavery, National Academy of Social Insurance, "When to Take Social Security Benefits: Questions to Consider," National Academy of Social Insurance, http://www.actuarialfoundation.org/pdf/nasi-final-brief-ss.pdf.

6. Jane M. Von Bergen, "Servant leadership in a financial crisis," *The Philadelphia Inquirer*, February 3, 2014.

7. Dinah Wisenberg Brin, "US retirement trails other nations'," CNBC.com on MSN Money, June 20, 2012, http://money.msn.com/retirement-plan/us-retirement-trails-other-nations-dinah-wisenberg-brin.

8. Thomas Stanley and William Danko. *The Millionaire Next Door: The Surprising Secrets of America's Wealthy*. (Atlanta, Ga: Longstreet Press, 1995).

9. Ibid.

10. Ibid.

11. Ibid.

12. Ibid.

13. James Randerson, "World's richest 1% own 40% of all wealth, UN report discovers," *The Guardian*, December 6, 2006, http://www.theguardian.com/money/2006/dec/06/business.internationalnews.

14. Thomas Stanley and William Danko. *The Millionaire Next Door: The Surprising Secrets of America's Wealthy.* (Atlanta, Ga: Longstreet Press, 1995.)

15. Ibid.

16. Ibid.

17. Ibid.

18. Statement of Thomas E. Perez, Secretary U.S. Department of Labor Before The Committee on Education and The Workforce, U.S. House Of Representatives, March 26, 2014, http://edworkforce.house.gov/uploadedfiles/dol_testimony_for_3-26_hearing.pdf.

19. Benjamin Graham. *Security Analysis.* (New York: McGraw-Hill, 2004).

20. Todd Bunton, "Are Dividends Important?" *Zacks*, March 7, 2014, http://www.zacks.com/stock/news/ 125679/Are-Dividends-Important.

21. Ibid.

22. Literature from Ideal-Living Expo, King of Prussia, PA. March 8, 2014.

23. Joel Kotkin, "America's Fastest-and Slowest-Growing Cities," *Forbes,* March 18, 2013, http://www.forbes.com/sites/joelkotkin/2013/03/18/americas-fastest-and-slowest-growing-cities/.

24. Brian Williams, "Pickleball: The Fastest Growing Sport in America," *NBC News*, March 18, 2014, http://www.nbcnews.com/watch/nightly-news/pickleball-the-fastest-growing-sport-in-america-199360067605.

25. *Neurology*, March 6, 2013.

26. Alzheimer's Disease International, Dementia Statistics, http://www.alz.co.uk/research/statistics.

27. Statistics About Diabetes, American Diabetes Association, http://www.diabetes.org/diabetes-basics/statistics/.

Notes

Notes

Notes

Notes